The Maci

The 290-mile Cc
across Fenland ai

*This book and the footpatl
memory of Douglas M
organisation now k.*

CW00739736

CONTENTS

Reproduced from Ordnance Survey mapping on behalf of The Controller
of Her Majesty's Stationery Office © Crown copyright MC 100014272

Published by
The Macmillan Way Association,
St Mary's Barn, Pillerton Priors,
Warwick CV35 0PG

© The Macmillan Way Association 2003

Printed and bound in Great Britain by
The Ancient House Press, Ipswich.

First published in its
present form - Jan 1st 2003

ISBN 0 9526851 4 0

Front Cover Photograph:

View of the Vale of Red Horse from
beyond Sunrising Hill *(see page 57)*

Introducing the Macmillan Way

This 290-mile, Coast-to-Coast, Long Distance Path and its branch path, Macmillan Way West have been developed to increase public awareness of Macmillan Cancer Relief and to assist in the raising of further funds for this vitally important charitable organisation, whose role is to improve the lives of people with cancer and their families.

In view of this, anyone walking all or part of the Macmillan Way can feel that they are walking *'Across Country for Cancer Care'*, as our waymark logo proudly proclaims. But at the same time they will be following a further, more geographical, theme as our trail has been planned to first cross the Lincolnshire Fens and then follow, as near as possible, the course of the long, oolitic limestone belt, which comprises stone known as 'Cotswold' in the Cotswold area, but which runs in slightly varying forms all the way from South Yorkshire to Dorset. The Macmillan Way starts from Boston and then runs across the Fens to their western edge at Kate's Bridge near Bourne before joining the limestone belt. From here it runs to Stamford and then along the shore of Rutland Water to Oakham. The Macmillan Way then heads south and west to Abbotsbury in Dorset, a coastal village noted, like Oakham, for its lovely old limestone buildings. Here then, once beyond the Fens is Macmillan Way's main unifying theme - a succession of delightful towns and villages, almost all of which are characterised by their warm, toffee- or honey-coloured stone, and all of which are set in gentle, typically English countryside.

Normanton Church, Rutland Water
(see page 30)

Like most long-distance paths, the Macmillan Way follows existing footpaths, bridleways and by-ways, and small stretches of minor roads when these are unavoidable. At times it shares its route with short lengths of a number of Regional Paths, such as the Leicestershire Round, Northampton-shire's Jurassic Way, Warwickshire's Centenary Way and South Somerset's Leland Trail, but for most of its length it is a truly original route. It provides a link in an existing chain of long-distance paths running from North Yorkshire to Oakham - the Cleveland Way, the Wolds Way and the Viking Way. It also links with the head of the Thames Path near Cirencester and with the South-West Coast Path at Abbotsbury. But perhaps the outstanding feature of the Macmillan Way is the rolling pastoral English countryside through which it passes - great tracts of quiet, unspoilt farmland, with views to distant skylines inviting the walker to go ever onwards. These farmlands are punctuated by great woodlands and secret, sunken paths overhung by trees, much as they must have been in medieval times. River banks and tree-shaded streams are often followed and hedges, many still not too ruthlessly trimmed, are usually alive with birds and small animals. No great climbs are required but when the flatter, rolling country ends, steep slopes lead up to ridge-tops from whence there are splendid panoramas ahead.

Our route sets out from Boston, along river and sea banks with views across the uniquely beautiful fenland country with its wide skies and the ever-present cries of birds, many of which nest in the reserves that are passed on the way. Once past Kate's Bridge, the fens are left behind and within a few hundred yards limestone can be seen on the surface of the already rising fields and this will never be far below the walker's feet for the rest of the journey down to Dorset. From Kate's Bridge the route goes across gently undulating countryside to the town of Stamford, the first and one of the finest, of the series of lovely stone towns through which the Macmillan Way passes.

Beyond Stamford the route leaves Lincolnshire, goes briefly through North-amptonshire, before entering the small, but justifiably proud county of Rutland. It soon follows the shore of the great reservoir of Rutland Water before arriving at Oakham. From here it sets out across the hilly Rutland

The Macmillan Way near Tunningham Farm (see page 50)

countryside, before passing into slightly lower Leicestershire. It then drops down to cross the Welland Valley back into greatly under-valued Northamptonshire. After running southwards over quiet farmland and along a disused railway line, it passes Cottesbrooke Hall, the fine gardens of Holdenby House and the great Althorp Park, before dropping down to Flore in the Nene Valley. Here it crosses the M1 motorway, the still busy A5, Watling Street and the Grand Union Canal before climbing gently onto the beautifully broad Northamptonshire uplands. Through a number of simple, unspoilt villages, past Canons Ashby House, and over old railway lines to wide-greened Chipping Warden. Now briefly into Oxfordshire and across the lovely Oxford Canal before heading into still-leafy Warwickshire, soon passing elegant Farnborough Hall with its grassy terrace overlooking a once quiet valley now disturbed by the busy M40. Beyond this it goes up onto the scarp that soon runs into Edge Hill, with its views westwards over the battlefield and the Vale of Red Horse to the distant Malverns. Here the Way passes close to Upton House, with its attractive sloping gardens and outstanding art collection.

Back briefly once again into Oxfordshire, with its toffee-coloured ironstone and a real flavour of the Cotswolds. Along Ditchedge Lane, an ancient green road with fine views, and then down into the Stour Valley and through woodlands before climbing up onto the true Cotswolds beyond Long Compton. Across high wold country, not far from the prehistoric Rollright Stones and past lovely Chastleton House before descending into the broad Evenlode Valley, with its memories of Jane Austen and Edward Thomas. Now in Gloucestershire, we climb once more up onto the wolds to pass close to historic Stow-on-the-Wold before descending into the Windrush Valley, to go through ever-popular Lower Slaughter.

From here we pass through many miles of classic Cotswold country, over high wolds and through a number of small villages, passing Chedworth Roman Villa before skirting the great Cirencester Park. Beyond this we go through great woodlands to emerge close to the old Thames and Severn Canal and the nearby source of the River Thames - the start of the Thames Path. Now west and south, over flatter country, passing to the north of Tetbury before walking right through the lovely Westonbirt Arboretum.

We now head southwards into quiet Wiltshire farming country, the peace of which is eventually much disturbed by yet another motorway

The Mill at Lower Slaughter (see page 67)

- the M4. But soon beyond this we start to follow the richly wooded By Brook Valley, first going through Castle Combe, once described as England's most beautiful village. We keep close to the By Brook as far as elegant Box, a village made famous by Brunel, who drove a long tunnel through its hill for his Great Western Railway. From Box we climb up onto higher country before dropping down into Bath's most elegant small neighbour, Bradford-on-Avon, with its fine old buildings including a unique little Saxon church. From here we follow the Kennet and Avon Canal for a mile or two before heading southwards up the Frome Valley, passing into Somerset beyond the manor house of Iford and the rugged castle of Farleigh Hungerford just beyond. Now up the Frome Valley before heading westwards towards the eastern Mendips, to skirt around Frome in a wide semi-circle.

We go down a deep wooded combe to Nunney's elegant castle and over flatter country at the head of the Frome Valley, before climbing up onto a ridge clad with the great woodlands of the Somerset and Stourhead estates. From Alfred's Tower, towards the southern end of this ridge, having perhaps first strayed from our route by walking down to Stourhead Gardens, we follow the Leland Trail, heading due west along an old road over flat country to the two delightful towns of Bruton and Castle Cary, both associated with Douglas Macmillan. We now climb out of Castle Cary, then through North Cadbury, across the busy A303 and below the great hill fort of Cadbury Castle, one of the legendary sites of King Arthur's *Camelot*. In hilly country to the south of Cadbury Castle we pass into our last county - Dorset - soon finding ourselves in the delightful old town of Sherborne, with its great abbey and two castles. From Sherborne our route passes through quiet farming country - Hardy's *Vale of the Little Dairies* - at the centre of which is little, stone-built Yetminster. However, this is soon left behind and we pass through the great park of Melbury before reaching the delightful village of Evershot.

From Evershot we walk southwards to Cattistock, on Dorset's River Frome. We follow this southwards to Maiden Newton before veering slightly east to enter chalk country for a mile or two, thus briefly deserting our limestone belt. In consequence we encounter beautiful open downland country and only return to the limestone within a mile or so of the sea at Abbotsbury, where old limestone quarries are clearly visible from our pathway above the village. And so, to St Catherine's Chapel, on its hill above the village and the final walk down to Chesil Beach beyond - the conclusion of our long journey across England.

How to Use this Guide

This guide to the 290-mile-long Macmillan Way is in two parts: The first, an introductory section giving some of the background to its creation and use. The second, a detailed description of the Way itself, divided into nine chapters, varying in length according to the appropriate stopping and starting points. The Key Map inside the front cover shows the way in which these chapters are split and which map numbers are covered in each chapter.

Each of the 58 double-page spreads is entirely self-contained, with map, text and possible illustration all inter-relating. This will ensure that when the book is opened out and inserted into a transparent map case, it can stay there until the next map section is reached. The maps are at a scale of 1:50,000 (about one-and-a-quarter inches to the mile) and are based upon the Ordnance Survey's Landranger series. The sheet numbers of the Ordnance Survey's Landranger and Explorer maps covering the area similar to that covered by each of our own maps are also noted. The symbols and conventional signs used on the maps are explained in the block below.

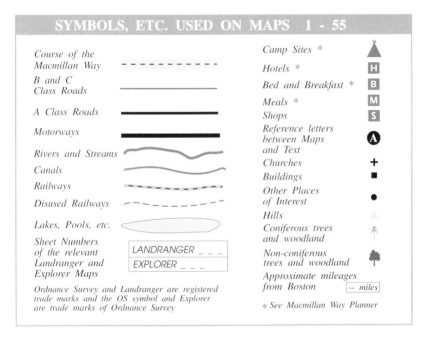

SYMBOLS, ETC. USED ON MAPS 1 - 55

Course of the Macmillan Way	– – – – – – –
B and C Class Roads	————————
A Class Roads	————————
Motorways	————————
Rivers and Streams	
Canals	
Railways	
Disused Railways	– – – – – – –
Lakes, Pools, etc.	
Sheet Numbers of the relevant Landranger and Explorer Maps	LANDRANGER _ _ _ EXPLORER _ _ _

Ordnance Survey and Landranger are registered trade marks and the OS symbol and Explorer are trade marks of Ordnance Survey

Camp Sites *	▲
Hotels *	H
Bed and Breakfast *	B
Meals *	M
Shops	S
Reference letters between Maps and Text	A
Churches	+
Buildings	■
Other Places of Interest	●
Hills	
Coniferous trees and woodland	
Non-coniferous trees and woodland	
Approximate mileages from Boston	-- miles

* See Macmillan Way Planner

Each paragraph of text starts with a reference letter and this cross-refers with the same letter on the accompanying map. All information not concerned with the main Macmillan Way route is shown in italics, while the route details themselves are in normal type. It will also be noted that progressive mileages from Boston are clearly displayed on every map and this will allow users to work out very simply the distance between any two points. It will also enable users to see how far they have gone and, by subtracting from the magic total of 290, to work out how far they are away from Abbotsbury. Perhaps this calculation should be avoided in the opening stages !

The 58 maps show the location of hotels, bed and breakfasts, meal places and

5

Dovecot at Chastleton (see page 63)

shops, either indicating their presence by being appended to the name of the appropriate town or village, or if well outside any town or village, their exact location. However bed and breakfast places do change from time to time, so always check the maps against the latest *Macmillan Way Planner*, which is frequently updated, and details of which are shown below. Also many village shops have closed in the last year or two and we cannot guarantee that our information remains entirely up-to-date.

With the help of this guidebook it should be possible to follow the Macmillan Way without further guidance. However, the route from Boston to Abbotsbury should also be waymarked, apart from sections using public roads and at one or two points where landowners have not been prepared to have our waymarks on their property. The waymarks are of two types - a self-contained plastic roundel with arrow and Macmillan Way logo, and a self-adhesive sticker with Macmillan Way logo, which is stuck on a standard yellow or blue waymark arrow (yellow for footpath and blue for bridleway). We hope that you have no difficulties, but if any are encountered it would be appreciated if you could let us have the details - *The Macmillan Way Association, St Mary's Barn, Pillerton Priors, Warwick CV35 0PG*. This will help us maintain the existing trail and improve it where necessary.

The Macmillan Way Planner

It will be noted that, apart from symbols on the maps, there is no information regarding accommodation in this guidebook. These details have been omitted as they date so quickly, but they are available in the frequently up-dated supplementary guide, *The Macmillan Way Planner*.

Amongst other items, this includes details relating to: Hotels, B&Bs, camping sites, pubs and restaurants on the route and Tourist Information Centres on or near the route. It also indicates in chart form, the relevant Ordnance Survey Landranger and Explorer Maps covering the whole route.

The Macmillan Way Planner is available from the *Macmillan Way Association, at St Mary's Barn, Pillerton Priors, Warwick CV35 0PG*. Please send a cheque *(made out to the Macmillan Way Association)* for a minimum of £2.75, all of which will be passed on to Macmillan Cancer Relief (if you wish to send more it would of course be gratefully received!).

Our Update Service - Don't Miss it !

A 290-mile long footpath is inevitably subject to certain small changes and with this in mind the Macmillan Way Association provides a free and frequently revised Update Sheet. To obtain this, please send a 22mm x 11mm, stamped and adressed envelope. Our address is above.

The South-North Supplement

We strongly recommend that the Macmillan Way should be walked **from** Boston **to** Abbotsbury, but in response to a number of requests, we have now also waymarked the whole route in the south to north direction. This route, from Abbotsbury to Boston, is described in a South-North Supplement, which provides route directions only and has no maps, illustrations or descriptions of places of interest. It is available from the Macmillan Way Association at £4.50 including postage (all of which will be passed to Macmillan Cancer Relief). But - think carefully before any decisions are made - the Boston to Abbotsbury direction is so much more attractive!

Walk Macmillan - Support Macmillan

The Macmillan Way has been developed as a tribute to Douglas Macmillan, the founder of the organisation now known as Macmillan Cancer Relief and it is being used by an increasing number of people who have discovered the particular pleasure of walking across country. If you haven't tried it yet - now is the time!

The Macmillan Way is helping to raise funds for Macmillan Cancer Relief and if you would like to help our ongoing campaign, might we suggest that you 'sponsor' yourselves for a small sum per mile and ask your friends and relations to help out by also becoming your sponsors. We can supply Sponsor Forms and would of course welcome your participation.

Certificates, Badges and Congratulations !

When you have finished your walk (either the whole route or, more likely, part of it) we could, if you wish, send you a Certificate of Congratulations. If you have managed to collect some sponsorship money (either from yourself, or from your friends and relations), this would be gratefully acknowledged on your Certificate. Do please remember to ask for a Certificate if you would like one, as we do not send them out automatically.

We are also able to supply cloth badges at a cost of £2.50 each. They are intended for those who have walked the whole of the Macmillan Way or Macmillan Way West or a substantial proportion of either. However some of those walking either of the Ways may like to identify themselves with a badge while en route and we would certainly not wish to discourage this. We leave the choice to you.

Congratulations on completing the Macmillan Way, or that section of it which you planned to complete. Do let us have your comments , both on the Way itself, and on the way we are organising it. They would be very welcome. Letters to: *The Macmillan Way Association, St Mary's Barn, Pillerton Priors, Warwick CV35 0PG.*

Douglas Macmillan's House, Castle Cary

Macmillan Cancer Relief

The Macmillan Way is dedicated to the memory of Douglas Macmillan, MBE, who founded the organisation now known as Macmillan Cancer Relief in 1911, following the death of his father from cancer.

Douglas Macmillan believed that by improving the knowledge of cancer among the public and health professionals, the needs of people with cancer would be better understood and their quality of life improved. His forward-looking vision still underpins the charity's work.

Macmillan Cancer Relief supports people living with cancer throughout the UK. The charity's aim is to help people from the moment they first hear that they have cancer, and to ensure that they get the best possible information, treatment and care.

There are now around 2000 Macmillan nurses and 300 doctors, working in hospitals and in the community. As well as supporting patients directly, they

Macmillan Nurse, Helen Lawrey

work closely with other health professionals, sharing their specialist knowledge and skills, to help improve standards of treatment and care for everyone with cancer.

Macmillan also helps people with cancer in other ways. The charity builds vitally needed treatment centres, gives financial help to those who need it most, and provide a range of cancer information both locally and nationally. You can find out more about the services Macmillan provides by calling the Macmillan Cancer Line on 0808 808 2020.

We hope that the Macmillan Way will help to raise awareness of Macmillan Cancer Relief, and to continue to raise money to fund Macmillan's much-needed services for people with cancer. Four in ten people in the UK will get cancer at some stage in their life and there are over a million people living with cancer - a figure forecast to double by 2020 - so directly or indirectly it affects us all. With your support, Macmillan can help people living with cancer.

Douglas Macmillan grew up in Castle Cary and used to walk to school in Bruton, almost certainly along paths that now form part of the Macmillan Way. We hope that you too will enjoy walking at least some of it.

The Macmillan Way is dedicated to the memory of Douglas Macmillan MBE, whose clan motto is, most appropriately, `I learn to succour the distressed'.

The Country Code

Enjoy the countryside and respect its life and work - Guard against all risk of fire - Fasten all gates - Keep your dogs under close control - *keeping them on leads when there is any chance of encountering stock. Don't forget that pregnant ewes are very much at risk even from merely playful dogs* - Keep to public paths across farmland *and walk in single file to minimise path-spread or crop damage* - Use gates and stiles to cross fences, hedges and walls - Leave livestock, crops and machinery alone - Take your litter home *(nice thought, but if you are some days away from home, dump it in a litter bin in the next village you pass through). Don't forget that litter is not only untidy, but it can also cause great harm to animals and farm machinery* - Help to keep all water clean - Make no unnecessary noise - Protect wildlife, plants and trees - Take special care on country roads, *usually walk towards oncoming traffic, but on blind bends walk on the outside of the bend where you will be most visible (we have tried to minimise the use of dangerous roads, but there are a few stretches which require great care).*

A Friendly Countryside for All

While planning the Macmillan Way we have received great kindness from many land owners and tenant farmers and we have assured them that walkers along our path will go quietly through their land and that you will not give offence. If you look at things from country people's point of view, they are far more likely to appreciate yours.

When meeting anyone on your journey, take time to stop and pass the time of day with them. Many farmers and farm workers to whom we have talked, say how surprised they are by the number of walkers who just plod by without even saying hello. Stop to talk and you could well learn so much more about the country through which you are passing. Don't be discouraged if you don't always get a response, but keep trying - the overall result will be well worthwhile, and the next Macmillan Way walkers that come along are more likely to have a friendly welcome. We have all got to live together, so please - let co-operation be your watchword, rather than confrontation. We are sure that you won't regret it.

Track beyond Little Brington (see page 46)

9

Chapter 1   Boston - Obthorpe   30 Miles

Apart from the number of pleasant old buildings, which remind us of Boston's prosperity as a port and market centre, places to visit naturally include the lovely St Botolph's Church. This is one of the largest and most impressive of England's parish churches, and memories of its lofty and beautifully proportioned interior could linger with you for the rest of your journey. Its impressive tower, topped by an octagonal lantern is known as Boston Stump and its 365 steps should be climbed for the outstanding views from its roof. The choir stalls are enriched by a very fine set of misericords (wooden brackets beneath the seats), carved with all the vigour and fun of medieval England. There is a memorial to Sir Joseph Banks, who sailed with Cook to Australia and also memorials to the many townspeople who sailed to the New World in the 1630s to found Boston, Massachusetts. Also, if possible, walk northwards to see the interesting and beautifully restored Maud Foster Windmill.

(A) Now, with a possible 290 miles ahead of you if you are heading for Abbotsbury on the Dorset coast, set out southwards from the Market Place with the handsome early 19th-century Assembly Rooms well over to its right, into South Street. Keep on South Street, crossing a number of narrow lanes, the remains of Boston's medieval street system. Pass well-restored half-timbered building on left, then Ship Inn and old Custom House. Spare a moment to walk to right for view from an old quay up to the Town Bridge and the Stump beyond. Now continue down South Street glancing to left down Spain Lane to see the Blackfriars Art Centre housed in an old Dominican Friary. Pass converted warehouse on right and Guildhall Museum on left. *Amongst many other interesting exhibits this contains cells in which the first group of Puritans were confined in 1607 after they had tried to flee to the Netherlands to escape religious persecution. It also contains the courtroom where they were tried after they had been betrayed by their Dutch sea captain, and arrested at Scotia Creek (see page 11). They were able to sail for Holland the next year, but it was some twelve years later that some members of this group set sail for the New World on the Mayflower and who later became known as the Pilgrim Fathers.* Now, on left, pass Fydell House, a handsome 18th-century Merchant's House, which is well worth visiting.

Turn right, cross the Haven Bridge beside the busy Inner Relief Road. Soon turn left (with great care) into High Street South, using the controlled pedestrian crossing and carry on down its left-hand side. River Witham soon to left, with a few boats alongside its wharves. Pleasant old Georgian buildings to right including the Ship Inn. Over railway level-crossing using pedestrian gates to left and onto pathway along river bank for a short while, still parallel with road. Back down onto footpath and over bridge crossing the South Forty Foot Drain. *This is one of the main channels draining the fens between Boston, Sleaford and Bourne. Its waters are emptied into the Witham by the massive Black Sluice Pumping Station, just to our right.*

(B) Immediately beyond bridge turn left through white kissing gate and go along sea bank with River Witham to immediate left. From here until the sea this tidal river is known as The Haven. Pass large storage silos on right and commercial quays and sheds over to left on far bank of The Haven, the latter not looking very busy. Over stile just before passing large electricity sub-station. Good view ahead left, over The Haven to the stout tower of Skirbeck Church. Easy walking along wide, grassy sea bank. Under very high, high-voltage power line which crosses the Haven here. *At about this point parts of the medieval sea bank are visible over to* *right. Until the New Sea Bank was built in the 1860s, the tidal marshes extended inland as far as the old bank and it was only then that the fields to our right were 'enclosed' and taken into cultivation.* **Over two stiles almost opposite Skirbeck Church.** *Good views back to Boston Stump, which will remain visible from our path for many miles to come.* **Passing large factory buildings well over to left, these lie to south of Skirbeck suburb.** *Now leaving busy Boston area and already starting to hear the haunting cry of sea-birds, as they fly along course of The Haven, to and from the Wash and its attendant marshes.* **Follow sea bank as it temporarily bears right, away from The Haven and then soon bears left again.**

(C) Over stile and start to pass area to right known as Slippery Gowt *(a 'gowt' is the Saxon term for a sluice, although there is no sluice here now)* with sea bank now becoming a grassy headland to a field to its immediate right. When large gate comes into view veer slightly left to keep on sea bank with thick, long grass (in summer and autumn) and not on track that becomes apparent during the last few yards. Pass waymark post by small bush. The large Slippery Gowt waste disposal area, with seagulls in vast quantities, now visible over to right. Keep on sea bank as it veers to left to come closer to The Haven. Open country now over to left. Start to pass high wire fence to right; probably intended to limit amount of rubbish being blown across The Haven. At end of wire fence, ignore tempting, roughly surfaced track which runs between the sea bank and the water, and keep to right, along sea bank, passing marker post on sea bank stating *Slippery Gowt.*

(D) Keep on sea bank as it veers to right, away from The Haven with boggy pools below left. Go through gate and keep along sea bank - now again more obvious. Over stile beside large wooden gate and keep straight ahead. Pass series of pools on left between sea bank and The Haven - grass shorter here. Over stile with Elkington's Farm visible well over to right. Through gateway and pass welcome line of poplar trees on right. Outfall from large sewage works well over to left. Over two stiles by track from Wyberton Marsh Farm (no access). *The Havenside Country Park just visible on far bank of The Haven. Before this area was drained, this was the site of Scotia Creek, the place where the first Puritan emigrants were betrayed by their Dutch skipper (see page 10).*

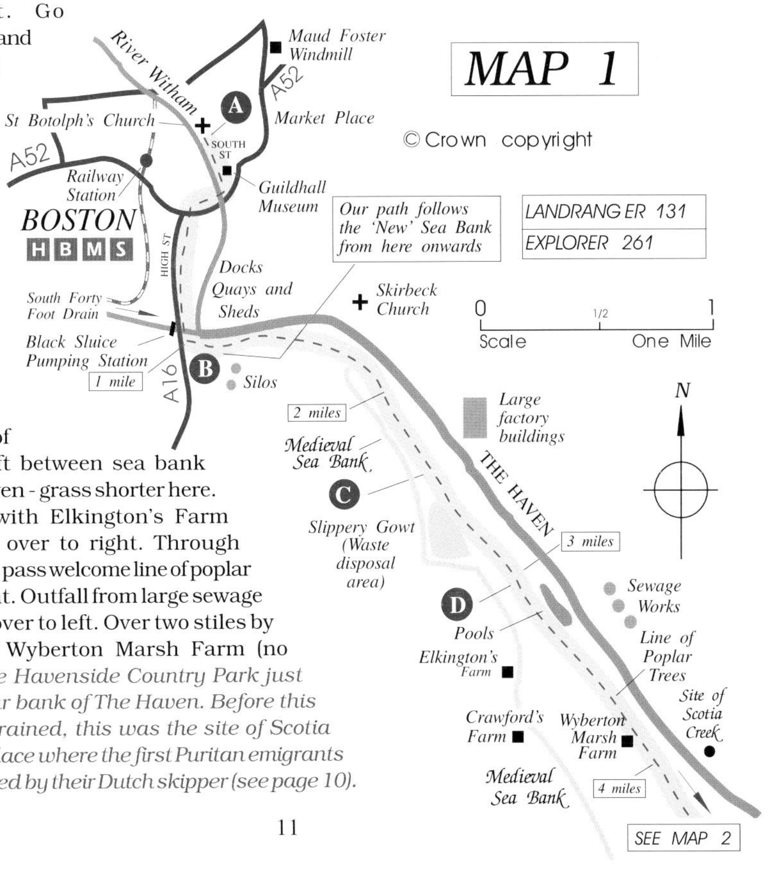

MAP 1

© Crown copyright

River Witham

A52

Maud Foster Windmill

St Botolph's Church

A
SOUTH ST

Market Place

A52

Railway Station

BOSTON
H B M S

HIGH ST

Guildhall Museum

Our path follows the 'New' Sea Bank from here onwards

LANDRANGER 131
EXPLORER 261

Docks Quays and Sheds

Skirbeck Church

South Forty Foot Drain

Black Sluice Pumping Station
1 mile

A16

B

Silos

2 miles

Medieval Sea Bank

C

Slippery Gowt (Waste disposal area)

D

Pools

Elkington's Farm

Crawford's Farm

Wyberton Marsh Farm

Medieval Sea Bank

Large factory buildings

THE HAVEN

3 miles

Sewage Works

Line of Poplar Trees

Site of Scotia Creek

4 miles

N

Scale 0 ... 1/2 ... 1 One Mile

SEE MAP 2

(A) Pass brick-built pumping station on right where The Haven starts to bend away to left. Follow sea bank as it takes sharp bend to right and then to left. Now start to leave bank of The Haven. Wide expanses of marshland open up to left, between our sea bank and The Haven, the first part being known as Wyberton Marsh, which runs into the much larger Frampton Marsh after a short time (see below). Do keep as quiet as possible all along the sea bank, so that disturbance to wildfowl and other birds is kept to a minimum. The pattern of drained, rich, cultivated farmland to right and marshland to left is now set for the next six miles. Walking still easy along this stretch of sea bank.

(B) Over stile and bear slightly left by track (bridleway) coming in diagonally from right. After about 100 yards, turn right at intersection of sea banks near to the possibly unsigned entry to Frampton Marsh Nature Reserve. *This is owned by the Royal Society for the Protection of Birds and covers 900 acres. This flat, tide-washed landscape is part of the Wash - one of the UK's most important estuaries for birds. Please remain on the sea wall (and of course keep dogs on lead) to avoid disturbance to wildlife, accepting that locals like to walk on the tidal marsh and collect samphire - a plant with salty and aromatic fleshy leaves, sometimes used in pickles. In late summer the marsh-lands are at their most colourful, with both sea aster and sea lavender in flower. Redshanks breed here in higher density than anywhere else in Britain and their attractive piping song is to be heard in spring and summer. Other breeding birds to be seen here include shelduck, oystercatcher, skylark, meadow pipit, reed bunting, linnet, mallard and short-eared owl. During spring and summer marsh harrier and whimbrel pass through here on migration. In winter the Wash is host to over 300,000 wading birds, ducks and geese many of which may be spotted from the sea wall here at high tide. Brent geese are to be seen, sometimes in flocks of over 5000. Dunlins, knots and bar-tailed godwits can also occur in large numbers and small flocks of twites, Lapland buntings and snow buntings are also be seen. (This information has been kindly supplied by the RSPB.) But whatever the season, the haunting cry of seabirds is almost always to be heard on this the landward edge of Frampton Marsh.* Turn right and then bear left keeping on sea bank.

(C) Bend round to right keeping on sea bank, now heading south-westwards. Pass small pool on right. Over stile and through gate near steps to right. *These steps lead down to path which soon becomes public road leading to vicinity of Marsh Farm. Limited car parking space here, used mainly by bird-watchers.* Follow sea bank as it gently curves first to right, then to left and then sharper right.

(D) Turn sharp left and not straight ahead along the Cross Bank. Almost immediately, through gate and onto a sea bank which may possibly be more overgrown. Through gate before sea bank begins to bend very acutely to left and head south-eastwards on this for a time.

(E) But soon follow sea bank as it bends almost ninety degrees to right and over stile beside large wooden gate onto sea bank with cropped grass. Follow sea bank as it veers slightly right and soon, by small pumping station, through two gates across track coming in from College Farm, visible over to right. *As in almost all Fenland the farming land soon started to shrink after it was drained as the usually peaty soil lost most of its moisture and it is largely for this reason that an elaborate network of pumping systems became necessary. These systems were first developed in the mid-17th century by Cornelius Vermuyden and others using an ever increasing number of windmills. However from about the 1820s these mills were gradually replaced by steam engines, followed in their turn by diesel and finally by electricity. The whole fascinating story may be followed at the Pinchbeck Engine Museum and the Ayscoughfee Hall Museum at Spalding (see page 16).*

(F) Over two stiles well to right of large wooden gates near point where public road comes in from right. There is limited car parking space here. Through gate and veer to left, and soon turn sharp right following sea bank. Bear left by pumping station and immediately bear left again making very acute change of direction. Good walking on well-mown or cropped sea bank. Passed blocked-off drain on right, which must have once been a tidal creek before the outer sea bank was built in about 1870. *Boston Stump still visible from here.* Now sea bank starts to gently curve to right as it begins to come closer to River Welland. Pass large pools on left and soon look over to the far bank of Welland, although at most states of tide, river itself does not become visible until sea bank runs much closer and almost parallel with it.

(G) Through hunting gate close to pumping station and start long, straight stretch. *Fine views back, north-eastwards, down Welland to the Wash, with light constantly changing in wide, open sky.* Marshland on either bank of the Welland gradually

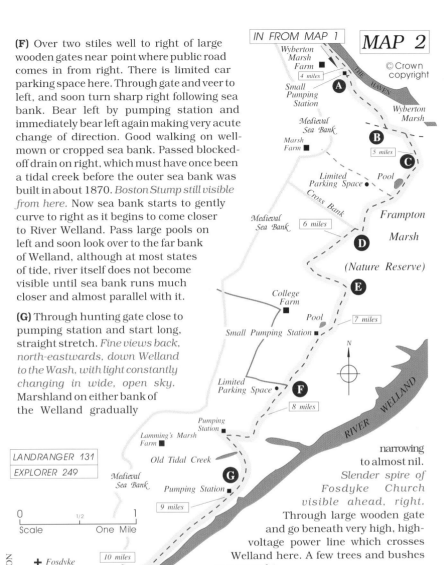

IN FROM MAP 1

MAP 2

© Crown copyright

Wyberton Marsh Farm ■
4 miles
THE HAVEN
Small Pumping Station
A
Wyberton Marsh
Medieval Sea Bank
Marsh Farm ■
B
5 miles
C
Limited Parking Space ●
Pool
Cross Bank
Frampton
Medieval Sea Bank
6 miles
D
Marsh
(Nature Reserve)
E
College Farm ■
Pool
7 miles
Small Pumping Station ■
N
Limited Parking Space ●
F
8 miles
RIVER WELLAND
Pumping Station ■
Lamming's Marsh Farm ■
Old Tidal Creek
G
Medieval Sea Bank
Pumping Station ■
9 miles

LANDRANGER 131
EXPLORER 249

0   1/2   1
Scale   One Mile

10 miles
✝ Fosdyke Church
H
Fosdyke Bridge
SEE MAP 3
■ Inn **M**
TO KING'S LYNN
11 miles

TO BOSTON
A17

narrowing to almost nil. *Slender spire of Fosdyke Church visible ahead, right.* Through large wooden gate and go beneath very high, high-voltage power line which crosses Welland here. A few trees and bushes now to right.

(H) Veer left and then right, following river bank as usual. Through hunting gate beside large wooden gate. At entry to Fosdyke Bridge and beyond, please keep as quiet as possible to limit disturbance to house owners. Pass bungalow (below right), cross concrete roadway and veer left on track and then veer right as track descends towards house and passes between houses on right and warehouses to left. Pass in front of office on right and through wooden gate with care. *The first Fosdyke Bridge was built in the early 19th century, but the present one is a relatively modern structure. There is a quay just to the seaward side of the bridge, and small coasting vessels can still be seen here from time to time.*

13

(A) If you wish to visit the nearby Ship Inn, turn left and cross bridge over Welland, *Otherwise cross busy A17 with very great care* and go down steps just along to right and on to surfaced roadway to immediate left of white-painted house and signed *Unsuitable for Motor Vehicles*. Up this track with Welland parallel to immediate left and pass Five Towns Pumping Station on right. Pass primitive landing stages on left and remains of meandering medieval sea bank now well over to right topped with bushes and small trees. Now on long, rather bland stretch of well-surfaced track running beside the Welland. Pass substantial Risegate Eau Pumping Station on right (built in 1964). *The word eau has no connection with the French word 'eau' as it derives from the old Norse word Aa, meaning water. An old fenman always pronounces the word 'Ea', which is no doubt correct. However most people in the area now say 'eau' as in the French. Confusing isn't it!* Track starts to gently curve to left. Pass Surfleet Marsh Farm on right.

(B) Pass Welland House Farm on right and through two gates beside cattle-grid. Track now starts to gently curve to right, away from the river. Just before going under high-voltage pylon line fork left off track and go onto bank beside River Welland. Through large wooden gate with small pumping station down to right. At entry to Surfleet Seas End village veer right, away from the Welland, keeping on river bank where the River Glen and Vernatts Drain (which drains pumped waters from Deeping Fen) can both be seen flowing into the Welland at sluice-gates ahead. Through kissing gate, pass many boats on landing stages below left and the hospitable little Ship Inn down to right, but remain on bank up to sluice gates at Point C. *Observant walkers will note that much of Surfleet Seas End is surrounded by banks (the writer first walked through without noting them at all !). These banks are the remains of Surfleet Reservoir, built in about 1740 as an experimental 'flushing reservoir', the first of a planned six. The idea was to collect water on the high tide and then to let it out in a rush, thereby flushing out the tidal mud which was impeding the navigation of the Welland between Spalding and the sea. It had to be abandoned as the mud settled out of the salt water and the reservoir soon silted up. Consequently the other five reservoirs were never built.*

(C) Through gap between hedge and gate and turn left onto public road. Cross bridge and sluice gate and immediately turn right down concrete steps onto path with River Glen now on right (now non-tidal). *The River Glen, with which we shall now keep company as far as Kate's Bridge, a distance of about 17 miles, is almost entirely isolated from the Fenland drainage scheme and is used to carry upland water across the Fens. The level of its banks is usually well above the level of the drained* land through which it *passes due to the latter's shrinkage (see page 20).* Pass bungalows on both banks of the Glen, then briefly on to concrete track. Soon turn right, over bridge crossing the Blue Gowt Drain *(a 'gowt', you may recall, was the Saxon term for a sluice).* Now veer to immediate left of

Boston Stump - the start of our journey (see page 10)

Low tide at Surfleet Seas End

bushes and immediately bear right passing shed on right to walk along bank of River Glen, with golf course to left. *The hills and hollows on the older parts of the golf course are the spoil heaps resulting from salt-making in medieval times.* **Note** warning sign stating: *Beware of golf balls. If a shout of 'Fore' is heard take evasive action.* 'Evasive action' does not necessary imply that walkers should immediately jump into the Glen, but it must be admitted that it is not easy to spot an oncoming golf ball. However, in practice, we feel sure that golfers will be reasonable when walkers are observed. Be prudent - keep as near the Glen as possible, eventually passing golf tee No 2. Towards end of golf course veer slightly left to pass to left of bungalow, joining track for a few yards. Then fork right and keep to right of miniature putting green to go right of fence to gate.

TO BOSTON

IN FROM MAP 2

Fosdyke Bridge

Five Towns Pumping Station

Medieval Sea Bank

Risegate Eau

Pumping Station ■

Inn ■ **M**

A

11 miles

TO KING'S LYNN

A17

Surfleet Marsh Farm ■

12 miles

Welland House Farm ■

B

© Crown copyright

MAP 3

Small Pumping Station ■

13 miles

Sea Bank

LANDRANGER 131

EXPLORER 249

14 miles **B** **M**

Inn ■

Sluice Gates

C

TO BOSTON

Surfleet Seas End

A16

N

B **M**

Hotel ■

SEE MAP 4

RIVER GLEN

Blue Gowt Drain

VERNATT'S DRAIN

RIVER WELLAND

Scale

0

1/2

One Mile

Golf Course

Club House

15 miles

TO SPALDING

15

(A) Go slightly right, down concrete steps and turn left to go under bridge carrying the busy A16 over the River Glen. Up steps beyond bridge with Riverside Hotel visible to right, across River Glen. (See note below regarding village stores, before going further.) Go onto very narrow headland between cultivated field and top of steep river bank. *(Note: There is a difference of opinion between the owner and Lincolnshire County Council, as to the existence of a right-of-way here, but for the moment the owner, Mr J A Dobney, has very kindly agreed to let Macmillan Way walkers use this narrow headland. Please ensure that you keep off the cultivated land to left but be careful not to fall down the river bank to right !)* Useful village stores visible across river to right - this could be reached from the bridge that we have just gone under - see above). Surfleet Church, with its extraordinary leaning tower and spire, coming into view ahead. A few houses to right and rich farmland stretching away to the left. At end of fields, veer slightly left, away from river bank, and through gap in hedge. Keep to right-hand edge of park-like garden with lawn and trees, then over stile and turn right on to minor road, just before crossing B1356, with bridge, Mermaid Inn and church all just along to right. *Not only does the 14th-century spire of Surfleet church lean at an alarming angle, but also the tower beneath it. However it has been in this state for many years and there appears to be no risk in looking inside, where there is a fine 15th-century font and the effigy of a knight.*

(B) Having crossed B1356, go down south (left) bank of River Glen to immediate left of bridge. Soon onto open bank with River Glen still to right. Look back for even better view of Surfleet's Church's leaning tower and spire. Good walking along wide grassy bank. *Between here and Pinchbeck West it is often possible to see fields of daffodils in the early spring. Years ago, the fields here were also colourful with tulips in late April and early May, but apart possibly for one or two fields specially grown for the Spalding Flower Parade, few tulips will now be evident.* Walk between cultivated field and river bank, which is a definite right-of-way. Path drops down on to terrace between bank to left and river to right. Path bends first to right and then to left, beneath shade of a number of cricket bat willows. *Despite enquiring locally we have no definite information as to when these willows were last used for the making of cricket bats.* Many wild duck usually to be seen on this stretch of river. Impressive tower of Pinchbeck Church visible ahead. Keep to right of wall and fence and soon over stile by bridge near Manor Farm, Crossgate, which is over to right. *(If you wish to visit the Pinchbeck Engine and/or the Spalding Bulb Museum, turn left onto road and use map to locate them.) The Bulb Museum tells the fascinating story of the Lincolnshire Bulb Industry and there are a number of other attractions including a coffee shop. The Pinchbeck Engine is a unique survival of one of southern fenland's steam powered pumping stations. Built as early as 1833, it continued working until 1952 and has now been restored to working order. There is also a Drainage Museum which tells the fascinating story of fenland drainage over the centuries.*

Spalding, which is about three miles south of here, is a busy market town with a number of elegant Georgian houses lining the River Welland, which flows right through its centre. It is the centre of the Fenland's bulb and flower industry and is the home of the famous Spalding Flower Parade, held each year during the first weekend in May. See especially Ayscoughfee Hall, which is now a museum telling the fascinating story of the reclamation of the fen country through which we are now walking.

(C) To resume our walk - go over second stile and along wall on left with industrial building beyond. Large water tower visible ahead. Where well-built limestone wall starts on left do not go through kissing gate to left but keep to right of wall. *(But go to left if you wish to visit Pinchbeck church - an ambitious building with a massive*

tower and an interesting interior including a fine nave roof with angels on its hammer-beams. There are several useful shops in Pinchbeck. Extensive housing estate to left - this is part of Pinchbeck village. At end of wall go slightly left into bushy area and down steps. Pass water tower on left and just before railway bridge, turn left over stile. Over railway line with very great care observing

Approaching Surfleet Church

sign stating 'STOP LOOK AND LISTEN'. Over second stile and walk across right-hand edge of car park of Ship Inn, Pinchbeck.

(D) Turn right onto public road beyond Ship Inn, cross bridge over River Glen and turn left off road immediately beyond. Walk along bank with River Glen now on left, and soon through hunting gate just beyond back of large truck garage on right. Tower of old windmill visible over to right. Through hunting gate and join minor public road known as Glenside North, which now follows right bank of River Glen. (We shall use this public road for the next two miles, but although rather bland, it is relatively quiet, as most traffic uses the parallel road on the south side of the River Glen.) Past entrance on right to 'Spalding Tropical Forest'. *This is believed to be 'the largest Tropical Forest in Britain' and, with its jungle foliage, cascading water and an atmosphere heavy with scents and blossoms, it provides a fascinating contrast with the Fenland landscape through which we are passing. There is a coffee shop, providing light lunches, teas and coffee.*

Pass the Woodland Trust's Pinchbeck Wood with grassy paths amongst alder, birch, ash and aspen. *The Trust is a cause well worth supporting.* Pass group of houses at Glenside on right. The Packing Shed Inn over to left, across the River Glen *(Walk ahead to Money Bridge and then back along opposite road if you wish to visit this inn, the buildings of which were once used for packing flowers).* Pass handsome Georgian House on right.

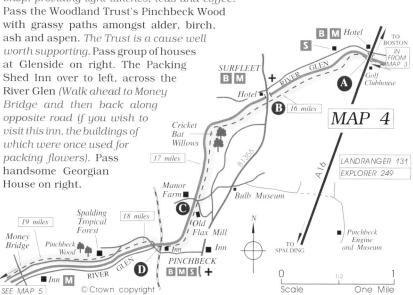

17

(A) Over X-rds at Money Bridge Lane continuing on Glenside North (but turn left and left again if you wish to visit Packing Shed Inn - about 200 yards). Soon pass telephone box on right . On a clear day, high ground to west of Bourne now visible beyond fenland, ahead right; the first we have seen since starting from Boston. Pass interesting remains of Glen Mill (windmill) on right. Straight, not right, by bridge at entry to Pinchbeck West, keeping on Glenside North.

(B) Turn left on to A151 in Pinchbeck West and over bridge with care. Cross road with care and immediately beyond bridge, before reaching the New Bridge Inn, turn right and over stile, to follow along top of River Glen's south bank. Now heading into much quieter countryside, although A151 still running parallel with us for a time, beyond north bank of the Glen. Walk along river bank, with Pinchbeck Slipe Nature Reserve between river bank and narrow lane to our left. Under low-voltage power line. Pass small bungalow farmstead of Glenhurst below left and soon over stile. Under another low-voltage power line. Pass Glenlea Farm below left. Pass another small farmstead below left (not named on map). This is fine open country, with good views to high ground beyond Bourne and large numbers of ducks and swans in River Glen. Pass two bird boxes on poles. *These are two of a whole series of boxes that we shall pass between here and Kate's Bridge. They were put up by the Hawk and Owl Trust and were intended for the use of barn owls, but regrettably only one or two have been used by the intended birds, the rest usually having been occupied first by kestrels, then by stock doves and finally by jackdaws.* Follow bank as it temporarily bends to left, away from River Glen.

(C) Go under low-voltage power line at Guthram Gowt *(this takes its name from Guthram, the Danish chief, who tried to occupy all England, but who, in AD879 was eventually forced by King Alfred to make a treaty known as the Danelaw, dividing the country between them. The area we are moving through remained very definitely in Danish hands. (A 'gowt', in case you had forgotten, is the Saxon term for a sluice). The South Forty Foot Drain (not visible) heads north from here, but does not connect with the River Glen. Both waterways were used by barges before the coming of the railways and goods were trans-shipped at this point.* Through gate on bank and bend left about 70 degrees. Pass small farms on both left and right and head southwards along bank, having finally shaken off A151. Pass bird boxes 35 and 36. Pass reed-lined pool down to left. Over fence just before bank veers left, away from

Beside the River Glen, near Tongue End

18

the Glen. Rich fenland country over to both sides, with dark, peaty soil and scattered farmsteads, most with at least a few trees surrounding them. Again note how much lower the land is here, due to shrinkage of the peat. Pass stone piers of a long-vanished railway bridge over to right, with an unusually large wood behind them on far bank. This bridge once carried the Bourne to Spalding Railway, a line which closed to passengers in 1959.

(D) Bend sharply round to right, to head along bank of the Glen south-westwards (which now continues with only slight variations, to the end of the fen at Kate's Bridge). Through large wooden gate and along close-cropped bank which provides easy walking. Through large wooden gate and pass two more bird boxes on far bank. Over stile where track comes in from left at point where Tongue End's council houses are visible over to left. Still more swans and ducks in this stretch of the Glen. Over stile and pass Bourne Eau Pumping Station (1964) on right, with small group of houses just beyond. *The Bourne Eau rises at the Well Head in Bourne and from the 16th to the mid-19th*

century was, apart from times when the springs ran dry, the final link in navigation between Bourne, Spalding and Boston, following the course of the Glen and the Welland, both of which were also navigable. It is hard to believe, but even beyond the point we have now reached, the Glen was also navigable by small craft as far as Kate's Bridge. Corn and wool were the main 'exports' to Boston and coal and groceries were 'imported'. As in most parts of the country, the coming of the railways in the mid-19th century effectively killed off this navigation, and in the 1860s a sluice was built here, blocking off any chance of further water-borne transport.

(A) Through wooden gate into short stretch of non-cropped grass and through second large wooden gate, with small farmstead below left. Through metal gate and cross public road with bridge to immediate right. This road connects Tongue End with Bourne. *The land between here and Bourne (South Bourne Fen) still has a covering of rich black peat and can support crops like celery and carrots. Due to the peat and its tendency to shrink over the years, there are almost no houses here, as the foundations have proved to be far too unreliable.* Through metal gate and along bank with River Glen still on right, and with long, non-cropped grass and attractive row of willow trees below to left. Under high-voltage power line. *Just beyond here, we cross the line of Sir Gilbert Heathcote's Tunnel. This was built in about 1630 and carried drainage water from Bourne South Fen under the Glen and into the Counter Drain, a drainage channel which still runs parallel to the Glen, over to our left. This tunnel was covered over some years ago and was finally demolished in about 1990.* Pass bird boxes 47 and 48. Now much closer to low hills ahead.

(B) Through metal gate where track from public road comes up from left and then over stile beside large wooden gate. Walking easier again as now back on close-cropped grass. Trees on left now more sporadic. Pass Windmill Farm, well over to left and, beyond it, also to left, a narrow belt of marshland with pools. *This is Baston Fen, a 90-acre reserve owned by the Lincolnshire Trust. Lying between the Glen and the Counter Drain, it consists of a long tract of permanent pasture, at the wooded end of which there were once eight cottages and a windmill. The whole area gives some impression of what the fenland must have looked like before drainage took place. In winter Baston Fen is flooded, and when thickly frozen, traditional fen skating takes place here. Over 160 species of birds have been recorded here, with shoveler, tufted duck, snipe, sedge warbler in the breeding season. In winter there are often as many as 1000 wildfowl here, including teal, wigeon and mallard, and occasionally Bewick's swan, pintail and goosander can be spotted. To visit the area properly, turn down left, opposite Windmill Farm and look at the information map displayed in the parking area. But, even when following our path beside the Glen, do ensure that dogs are kept on leads.*

Over stile by wooden gate. Although its banks remain just as high as before, the Glen is now becoming ever narrower and shallower and occasionally we pass small makeshift dams of turf and stone, put there to help with summer irrigation. Pass bird boxes 49 and 50, the last we shall encounter. Over stile beside wooden gate.

(C) Pass Poplar Tree Farm, well over to left and pleasant small plantation over to left just beyond. Over stile beside gate and Baston church tower soon just visible over to left. Noise of traffic on busy A15 ahead can now be heard. Pass attractive wood well over to left. Through gate and veer left over stile beside second gate to follow a long semi-circular loop temporarily leaving the Glen, but still on raised bank. Pass waymark post. Pass boggy drain to right, with willows, and then between trees on both sides. Thetford House Farm just visible through trees over to left. Pass another waymark post, then immediately over stile by wooden gate and turn left to re-join the Glen. Just beyond, over stile by second gate and keep on high bank which

Kate's Bridge - on the edge of the Fens

briefly veers away from the Glen. The buildings of Kate's Bridge Farm just visible over to right where the bank re-joins the Glen. *At about this point we cross the line of the Car (or Carr) Dyke, although there is no sign of it here. This channel, which ran between Waterbeach in Cambridgeshire to the Witham near Lincoln, was cut by the Romans, almost certainly as part of a fenland drainage scheme. Some believe that it was also used by them for water transport, but this is not probable.* On going up final fenland field, note height of bank which gets lower in relation to field as the latter gradually gains in height - evidence that the need for special fenland drainage is receding with every step we take. Note first simple bridge just ahead and to its right, the elegant stone-built Kate's Bridge. *This is almost certainly an 18th-century structure, but there was a bridge here as early as 1349, known then as 'Katebrigg' or 'Catebrigg' and it is thought that `Ket' (or `Kat') was probably a local Danish deity.*

Go through gateway and turn right on to the 'old main road', to go over small bridge and then over Kate's Bridge. (Turn left here if you wish to walk with care to Waterside Garden Centre - lunch, coffee, teas - 1/4 mile south - see map.) *At this point a Roman road, which ran northwards, roughly parallel with the more important Ermine Street, and known latterly as King Street, crossed the River Glen, almost certainly by a ford. It is possible that it was built in conjunction with the Car Dyke. Here, for the moment, we leave our friend the River Glen, and say goodbye to the wonderfully remote Fenland country across which we have been walking.*

(D) Cross the ever busy A15 with very great care and follow footpath waymark to go to immediate left of small, V-sectioned drainage ditch. *(If leaving route for accommodation, there should be frequent buses to Thurlby from here.)* Keep on very narrow headland on left side of ditch as it gently curves to right, and even rises a foot or two - quite a shock after our long fenland journey! *There appears to be some loose limestone in the fields here - reminding us that, from here onwards, almost all of the Macmillan Way follows this, as its theme, on its long journey across England to Abbotsbury.* Soon join wider headland heading to immediate left of farmhouse ahead (Obthorpe

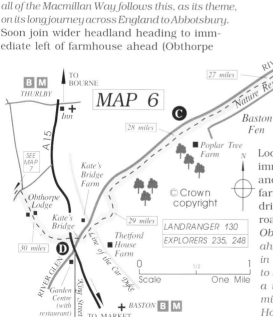

Lodge). Go across farmyard to immediate left of farmhouse and carry straight on up long farm drive. At end of farm drive, turn left onto public road at junction of roads (SP - *Obthorpe*). *(But go straight ahead up road and turn right in Thurlby village if you plan to stay at B&B here, which is a total distance of under a mile and not far from the Horseshoes Inn.)*

21

(A) Walk down road, below high-voltage power line, through Obthorpe, a hamlet with no special features, and keep on road beyond it. After one mile, bear left at road T-junction (SP - *Wilsthorpe*) and soon enter the small village of Wilsthorpe. Straight, not right, at junction in village (SP - *Greatford*) and pass telephone box on left. Turn right, off road just before reaching church on left. *This handsome little early 18th-century building is quite unusual and has a pleasant interior, despite restoration by over-enthusiastic Victorians. A certain Mr Parkinson scraped his name on a wall within the west end of the church in 1759, thus proving that vandalism is no new thing !*

(B) Down short driveway between houses and over stile to cross small paddock diagonally left to next stile. Over this stile and keep in same direction aiming for bridge just to left of pylon, near left-hand corner. *(Braceborough church spire visible over to right.)* Over first bridge and then, after crossing ditch, keep in same direction, aiming for single willow tree with second bridge beside it. Bear left over this bridge crossing the East Glen River - *this is joined by the West Glen River about half-a-mile to east of here and the resultant River Glen then flows north-eastwards to Kate's Bridge.* Bear right beyond bridge and cross track to head diagonally across large field aiming well to right of first woodlands. Over sleeper bridge at end of field and turn right to follow along edge of field with hedge to immediate right. Keep along edge of field, turning left in corner and skirting around small wood on right. Continue along edge of field with hedge still to right and go straight, not right, ignoring bridge in hedge to right, and about 115 paces beyond bridge, turn left onto initially narrow headland between fields (no hedge) by lone ash tree. Aim to left of red-roofed house on edge of village.

West doorway, Wilsthorpe Church

(C) At end of headland, now more like a track, go straight ahead joining public road at entry to Greatford. After about 200 yards turn right into Greatford Gardens (a surfaced roadway) *(but go straight ahead and soon turn right if you wish to visit the Hare and Hounds Inn and/or the church). Greatford is a pleasant stone village astride the little West Glen River, with a fine Elizabethan house close to a much-restored church. Within this building will be found two monuments, one by the fashionable sculptor, Nollekens, to members of the Willis family, who had private lunatic asylums both here and at neighbouring Shillingthorpe Park. It was this family, father and sons, who cured George III of his bouts of madness.* Straight, not right, to follow roadway between weeping willow on left and conifer trees on right. Pass small transformer station on left and soon turn right in front of wrought iron in front of wrought iron gates. Now on narrow pathway and across left-hand side of lawn (*please keep as quiet as possible - this is part of a private garden*). Over wooden footbridge and turn left into narrow belt of woodland with willow trees lining ditch not far beyond on left. Turn right at end of woodland and over stile to go up field with hedge and trees to immediate left. Soon turn half-left to cross field diagonally, passing remains of old pond to left. Cross line of ditch and veer slightly to left to cross field with lone oak tree in middle of field, on left. Over stile just beyond three oak trees in a group on edge of field and veer diagonally right to head up narrow field to top left-hand corner.

(D) Over stile and just beyond, turn left onto track lined with trees and bushes. Soon through metal gate and keep down track across field which is part of the old Shillingthorpe Park (*the house, once used as a lunatic asylum by the Willis family, was demolished some years ago*). Go over bridge crossing the West Glen River and head up track (*this is the last time that we shall encounter our old friend the River Glen*). Veer slightly right to go up track below avenue of trees, soon over stile beside metal gate and turn right onto public road. Keep on this road for 1¹⁄₂ miles - it is fairly quiet and has a wide verge. But beware of crossing very fast railway line about half way along this road - STOP, LOOK AND LISTEN - if the warning lights are flashing, do be patient and wait for train (or trains) to pass.

(E) About 500 yards beyond Rutland entry sign turn left at T-junction (SP - *Uffington*). Very soon turn right, off road, onto narrow and often rather muddy 'green lane' with overhanging trees and bushes. *Now following the boundary between the counties of Rutland (to our right) and Lincolnshire (to our left).* Gradually climb up this green lane, passing Seven Acre Wood on left and eventually levelling out at a height of about 150 feet above sea level - by far the highest point of our journey so far! Keep on track, ignoring footpath signs to right and left.

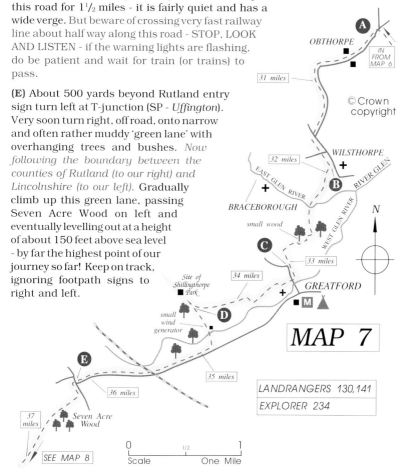

OBTHORPE

IN FROM MAP 6

A

31 miles

WILSTHORPE

32 miles

EAST GLEN RIVER

BRACEBOROUGH

B

RIVER GLEN

WEST GLEN RIVER

N

small wood

C

33 miles

34 miles

Site of Shillingthorpe Park

GREATFORD

M

D

small wind generator

MAP 7

E

35 miles

LANDRANGERS 130,141

EXPLORER 234

36 miles

37 miles

Seven Acre Wood

SEE MAP 8

0   1/2   1

Scale   One Mile

23

(A) Soon emerge onto public road by bearing slightly left by the entrance drive to Cobbs Nook Farm on left. Keep in same direction down road for about 200 yards and then turn right, off road. Now back into Lincolnshire and over stile just beyond and, keeping in same direction, go diagonally left down field. Initially aim to left of left-hand of two spires - our first, but certainly not our best view of the lovely town of Stamford. Now aim for left-hand end of large industrial building and stile soon comes into view. Over this small stile to left of water trough and keep in same direction. Over bridge crossing River Gwash, *which flows into the River Welland not far south of here, and which also flows 'through' the great reservoir of Rutland Water. We shall encounter it again beyond Oakham.* Initially veer left in meadow to keep beside Gwash to left but after about 100 yards veer right, away from river heading towards far, right-hand end of field, and aiming for latticed mast. Over rudimentary stile in corner of field, through gap in disused railway embankment (once a bridge) and up track between industrial buildings - a somewhat inauspicious entry to Stamford.

Stamford, regarded by many as 'the finest stone town in England', is the first of a whole series of stone towns through which the Macmillan Way runs. In medieval times and beyond, its prosperity was based largely upon wool and its trade in this and other commodities especially with the merchants of Calais. This trade eventually declined, but thanks in part to its position astride the Great North Road Stamford remained comfortably off and many fine Georgian buildings now line its medieval streets. Although many Stamfordians grumbled at the time, the lack of an early railway connection saved it from the worst excesses of the Industrial Revolution and today the town retains a quite unique flavour of past times.

There are a bewildering number of places to visit and we would suggest that you call at the Tourist Information Centre (see below) to obtain a helpful map of the town. In Broad Street, parallel to the High Street, through which we pass, will be found the ancient almshouses known as Browne's Hospital and also the town's interesting museum. We pass All Saints Church, with its beautifully timbered chancel roof complete with painted angels, but see also the fine churches of St Mary and St George, both close to the TIC, and the church of St Martin, south of the Welland and beyond the historic George Hotel. If time allows, also visit the interesting Steam Brewery.

(B) Turn left onto busy road (A6121, but not indicated here) with factories to left and houses to right. Cross road (with care) as soon as possible, keeping in same direction and heading towards town centre. Pass sub-post office on left, ambulance station on right and hospital on left. At mini-roundabout bear right into St Paul's Street. Go straight across busy X-rds keeping on St Paul's Street (not signed at this point). Now entering the older and much more attractive part of Stamford. Carry on down St Paul's Street and into High Street, which is pedestrianised and which has many modern shops. Walk straight along High Street, passing handsome Public Library with classical front on right, pass turning on left to Arts Centre and Tourist Information Centre, and (unusually) church on left converted into shops.

(C) Pass HSBC Bank on right and over busy road at end of High Street into Red Lion Square with tall-spired All Saints Church up to right. Go ahead for a few yards and then bear left down Horseshoe Lane. Keep straight across wide road junction and down Castle Dyke (road). Go over footbridge crossing narrow stream (a minor branch of River Welland) and go diagonally right by squat stone pillar signed *Vence Walk. Although neither are waymarked hereabouts we are now on both the Hereward Way and the Jurassic Way. The Hereward Way runs from Peddars Way in Norfolk to Oakham and we shall share most of its route from here to Oakham. The Jurassic Way is a well-waymarked Northamptonshire County Path, running for 88* *miles between Stamford and Banbury in Oxfordshire. The Macmillan Way not only follows it between here and Ketton, but also joins it between Brampton Ash and Great Oxendon, and between Eydon and Chipping Warden.* Through gate by picnic tables beside River Welland to left - look back here for fine views of Stamford. Head across next meadow keeping fairly close to River Welland on left.

(D) Through gateway with Welland just to left and squat stone pillar to left marking the point where the Roman's Ermine Street probably crossed the River Welland, with plaque stating *One of the most important Roman roads to the north, from London to Lincoln and York, crossed here. In AD61 survivors of the Ninth Legion fled this way, pursued by Queen Boadicea. After the collapse of the bridge the lower crossing was preferred and the first town of Stamford grew around this in Saxon times.* Now veer right, away from the Welland for a while, but then keep parallel with it, heading across large meadow on well-used path, which loosely follows lower-voltage power line. Over Broadeng Bridge crossing River Welland, and turn right immediately beyond. *(Jurassic Way waymarks now occur frequently.)* Follow path beside willow-bordered Welland, now on our right. Veer left away from Welland and head for underbridge beneath noisy A1 road.

(E) Go beneath A1 and carry on in same direction beyond sleeper bridge over ditch. Up over wooden footbridge crossing boggy area and cross busy, curving railway line with extreme care, as curve prevents long view, observing Railtrack's notice stating 'STOP, LOOK AND LISTEN'. Over second footbridge crossing boggy area (entering Northamptonshire at about this point)

and emerge from overgrown area to go straight up field on well-used path. Now on steeper track passing young oak trees to left and extensive wood to right. Now pass open field to left and hedge with oak trees on right. Leave track where it bends to left and go straight across field on well used path. Over stile in hedge and keep in same direction across small corner of field. Over stile into turfed area with beech hedge to left, across drive through gateway to enter Easton-on-the-Hill.

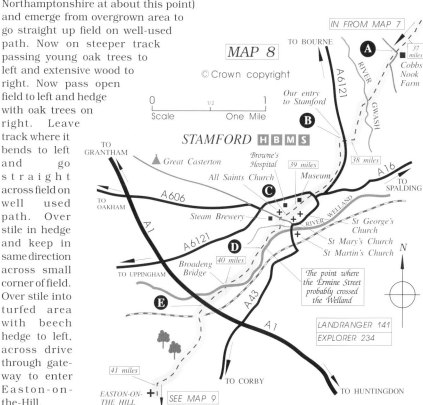

25

(A) Through small gateway and turn left on to public road (Church Street), soon passing Easton-on-the-Hill church on right. *Easton-on-the-Hill is a delightful stone village, well sited above the Welland valley, with many attractive houses and cottages, including the National Trust's Priest's House, a small early 15th-century priest's lodge, which is only open by appointment. Its large, partly Norman church stands in a tree-shaded churchyard. Light floods into its very pleasant interior through many windows of clear glass and there is much 17th-century woodwork to be seen.* Soon enter village with its many attractive stone houses and cottages. Straight, not right, keeping on Church Street, and pass phone box and Post Office Stores on right. Turn right into High Street by War Memorial and pass Blue Bell Inn on right. Over X-rds just beyond and into Westfields Road. Pass useful general stores on left and soon onto track known as Ketton Drift, where public road bends to left, with phone box on right. Pass playing field on left and the vast Ketton Cement Works now visible over to right. Fork left off track as this veers to right and over stile. Head diagonally left across field dropping gently towards valley and through gap in hedge with waymark post, with trees in field below to right. Keep in same direction across next field, now dropping more steeply and through gap in hedge below oak tree. Keep in same direction across next field and through gap in hedge with small bridge and turn right onto public road.

(B) Over Collyweston Bridge crossing the River Welland and into the county of Rutland (soon signed on right). Pass line of trees away to right, keep on road out of valley which soon bears right by Ketton entry sign. As fingerpost here indicates, *(We now leave the Jurassic Way, but continue following the Hereward Way.)* Go straight, not left, leaving wider road by doctor's surgery at entry to Geeston hamlet. Turn left just beyond bungalow named *Newnham* and, after 20 yards, fork right onto path through bushy area. Over footbridge crossing railway line, along path and over roadway in housing estate in Aldgate hamlet and then down narrow pathway between Leylandii hedge and fence. Over stile and keep across field in same direction. Bear left at real entry to Ketton onto public road and over footbridge to right of old three-arch stone bridge with cutwaters, crossing the little River Chater. Good view of tall-spired Ketton church just beyond. *Ketton is a large village, somewhat overshadowed by the massive cement works just to its north. However it has a number of pleasant stone houses and cottages and an impressively large church with tall spire and an unusual west-end with a rounded Norman central arch flanked by two later, pointed arches, all with dog-tooth decoration. Its interior is equally impressive, especially the arches beneath the tower crossing.*

Stamford from the River Welland (see page 25)

Pass church on right and turn right just beyond the Railway Inn to go up Chapel Lane, which becomes narrow pathway. Turn left onto road and almost immediately bear right onto small road. *(We now leave the course of the Hereward Way for a short distance.)*

(C) Turn right onto A6121 road (not indicated here), cross over to left-hand side by police house and keep down A6121 for about 500 yds. Pass library and school on right and turn left off A6121 just beyond bench and village notice board and just short of useful Post Office Stores. *(But go straight ahead for a short distance if you wish to visit the Northwick Arms.)* Through farmyard of Home Farm. Keep to left of buildings and go up short farm track. Go left through gateway near dutch barn to right and up long farm track with hedge on immediate right, gradually climbing all the way. *(It is probable that there will be a west-looping diversion to left to avoid new quarrying - follow waymarks as indicated - to eventually rejoin route.) (Further diversions are threatened - see latest Update Sheet) (We re-join the course of the Hereward Way, which comes in from left. at about this point)* Through gateway keeping on track and ignoring fingerpost pointing right to quarry. Pass dutch barn on left and start to descend. Vast quarry now visible well over to right.

(D) Our track now shaded with a few trees but where track veers to right by old windpump, go straight ahead through gap in fence to cross field in same direction as previously, aiming for waymark in cross-hedge. Over stile and veer slightly right heading for far right-hand corner of next field. Ignore bridleway waymark by hunting gate to right. Over stile by large wooden gate in corner of field and keep in approximately same direction across next field, aiming for waymark post at right-hand end of New Wood. Through gap in hedge to immediate right of New Wood and to left of long, very narrow plantation and aim for waymark post to right of trees and buildings of Woodside Farm. Pass farmyard on our immediate left and keep in same direction aiming for gateway in hedge ahead.

(E) Over stile beside metal gate at public road, but immediately turn right off road, to go through metal gate and down field keeping to immediate left of hedge. Good view of Empingham ahead, on far side of the Gwash Valley. Pass Ling's Spinney on our right as we start to descend slightly. Through metal gate and still keep to immediate left of hedge.

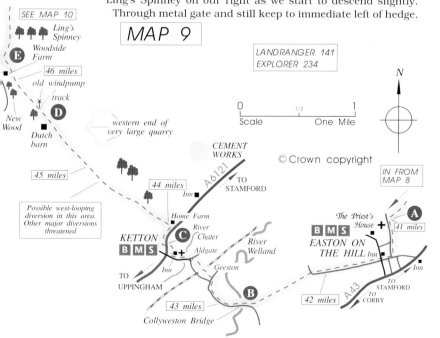

SEE MAP 10

Ling's Spinney

Woodside Farm

E

46 miles

old windpump

track

D

New Wood

Dutch barn

western end of very large quarry

MAP 9

LANDRANGER 141
EXPLORER 234

N

0   1/2   1
Scale   One Mile

CEMENT WORKS

IN FROM MAP 8

45 miles

Possible west-looping diversion in this area. Other major diversions threatened

44 miles

Inn

A6121

TO STAMFORD

Home Farm

River Chater

C

KETTON
B M S

Aldgate

River Welland

Geeston

The Priest's House

B M S

EASTON ON THE HILL   Inn

A

41 miles

Inn

TO UPPINGHAM

Inn

B

42 miles

A43

TO STAMFORD

TO CORBY

43 miles

Collyweston Bridge

(A) Through gateway, cross the busy A606 with care and through gateway opposite. Keep down field dropping down into valley still keeping to immediate left of hedge. Through metal gate and beneath high-voltage power-line to go through another metal gate, still keeping to immediate left of hedge. Ignore footpath signs on stile to right and at end of field veer slightly left to go over metal footbridge crossing the meandering River Gwash. Beyond bridge veer right and aim to right of small house which was probably once a watermill and bear left onto track immediately beyond it. Through white-painted 'gateway' and beyond transformer on pole, over stile to left onto path. Over wooden footbridge crossing the little tree-shaded North Brook and across field, veering slightly right and aiming towards waymark post by right-hand of two houses ahead.

(B) Over stile and onto tarmac path in front of houses at entry to modern part of Empingham. Soon bear left at road junction in direction of church spire, but bear right up next road beyond house on right called *The Rowans*. Immediately over small X-rds and turn left just beyond house on left signed *No 1*. Go down narrow path and through metal kissing-gate and soon join public road with stone and thatch cottages on either side. Bear left into Crockett Lane (not indicated here) by Peartree Cottage on left, again heading for church. Pass two fine weeping willows on right and soon pass church on left. *Empingham is a pretty stone village poised on slopes above the little River Gwash, here fresh from its exit from Rutland Water. There are several pleasant houses here, but the most impressive is the Prebendal House, a fine, late 17th-century building with an elegant front (see below). Like Ketton, Empingham has a large church with impressive spire, this one poised above an exceptionally fine 14th-century tower. Inside will be found a delightful triple sedilia and piscina and there are fragments of medieval glass in the north transept windows.* Turn left by churchyard gate onto Church Street and pass antiques shop and village shop on right. Prebendal House up to left.

(C) Bear right just beyond to go onto little green overlooked by houses lining Audit Hall Road, but this merges with the ever busy A606. Keep on path beside A606, but after phone box on right, cross A606 with great care where it bends to right, taking first road off to left, which is Nook Lane and which is signed (for motorists) 'No Access to Rutland Water'. *(But carry on up the A606 for 150 yards if you wish to visit the White Horse Inn.)* At T-junction beyond Nook Cottage, go straight ahead onto grassy walk between garage on left and house on right. Through gate and veer diagonally left down field to go over stile in bottom left-hand corner. The Rutland Water dam is now a feature of the skyline ahead - just a straight line! *(From this point onwards our route along the north shore of Rutland Water is owned by Anglian Water and is a permissive one only. Please follow the Cycle Path signs closely, remembering that Macmillan waymarks will probably not be displayed for the next four miles.)* Over stile and turn right to follow to immediate left of short fence. Soon over stile in wooden fence ahead and over small wooden bridge crossing minute stream. Up short meandering path which soon heads through bushes in straight line to right. At end of bushy area over stile and keep in same direction across field aiming for gateway just to right of old Ordnance Survey trig point (concrete pillar). The large sweep of grassland below the dam top gives a pleasant impression of open downland. Through large metal gate and follow up field keeping close to fenceline on right. Near top of field aim for large noticeboard visible on right-hand end of dam, thus eventually veering away from the fenceline to right.

Beneath its grass cladding this dam is built largely of clay and behind it lies the 3,100 acres of beautiful Rutland Water, the largest pumped-storage reservoir in Europe. It takes its water from the Nene and Welland rivers and is a major element in the strategic Ruthamford Water Supply System. At the same time it provides a series of leisure facilities, including a 25-mile cycle path around its shores, part of which we shall now be using. Details of this and all the other Rutland Water facilities including nature trail (see below), bird-watching, fishing, passenger cruising, sailing, windsurfing, canoeing) are available at the Information Centre at Sykes Lane , near our main route, just beyond the dam (open daily April - October and weekends November - March). Also ask here for details of the project to establish ospreys here.

(D) By metal notice, bear right onto cycle path which goes along the dam top and soon bear left through metal gate. (But turn sharp left onto cycle path if you wish to start South Shore Option - move to top of page 30.) Main route now goes through the metal gate to enter Sykes Lane Park Area. Well over to right there are: Butterfly and Aquatic Centre, Information Centre, toilets and refreshment facilities, but if none of these services are required we suggest you veer left as soon as possible to walk below the trees just inland from the shore. At end of parking area turn right by 'The Great Tower' an impressive bronze sculpture just above shore and keep woodland on left before turning left onto surfaced cycle path and going through small gate just beyond. *Feature in water well over to left is the Limnological Tower, which contains instruments for measuring water temperature and quality.* The cycle track can be followed to the Whitwell Lodge Area, but walkers may prefer to keep closer to the shore and to stop awhile by bench beneath clump of trees overlooking Whitwell Creek, usually busy with sailing craft. From here it will be necessary to head up right to rejoin cycle track before heading round north end of creek.

(E) Bear left at T-junction just inland of Whitwell Creek and soon pass large boat storage area on right with the creek down to left. Only go straight ahead if you wish to visit Whitwell Lodge Watersports Centre and other amenities (*including the Rutland Belle passenger cruiser, fishing boats and bar/cafe*). Otherwise bear right up hill, passing car park hut on left, turn right onto wider roadway and almost immediately turn left, passing small box signed ` *Catch Returns'*. Head towards cycle hire shop but then veer to its left and soon bear right to pass between Crafty Fox Cafe and toilet block. Now follow cycle track *(which also serves as a nature trail between here and Barnsdale car park area - leaflet available from Information Centre)* as it soon bends round to right, through small metal gate and down into dip before going up again. Pass seat on left overlooking Barnsdale Creek, near a stone with a memorial plaque to Dame Sylvia Crowe, the landscape architect of Rutland Water. Now follow cycleway to plunge into woodlands, soon passing bird hide down to left overlooking shoreline and a platform for the same purpose. Now turn to top of page 32.

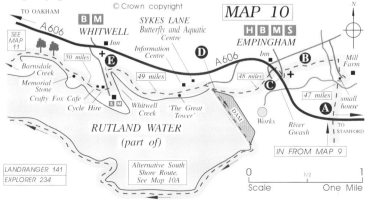

© Crown copyright

MAP 10

29

(A) Having come up the sloping grass wall of the Rutland Water dam on Map 10 (page 29), turn sharp left at the top and go on the cycle track along the top of the dam. *Note: Keep on cycleway until reaching the Lyndon Nature Reserve. As this is an alternative route, there will be no Macmillan Way waymarks.* Fine views right across Rutland Water. At end of dam bear round to right going through two small metal gates crossing surfaced drive and passing valve tower on right (SP - *Normanton*). Our route uses cycleway, but often possible to walk closer to shore.

(B) Pass entrance on left to the Normanton Park Hotel, including 'The Sailing Bar' for drinks and ice creams. Pass 18th-century Normanton Church down to right, which has been protected from the water by an encircling dam and has its floor raised by many feet. Try to visit the interesting museum here with its video telling the fascinating story of the reservoir's construction. There are also displays relating to Rutland Water, to Anglo-Saxon discoveries made during construction work and to nearby Normanton Hall, which was demolished in 1926. *The museum and shop are open daily from end March to end October.* Pass pontoon down to right, which is one of the stopping points for *The Rutland Belle* passenger cruiser. At end of mown section bear slightly right to go across track into grassy area *(but turn left up here if you wish to visit Edith Weston village).* Over stile and immediately bear left into car park passing fishing harbour down to right. Pass to left of The Tickled Trout Bar and Restaurant and up surfaced road before bearing right to go to right of toilet block. Soon bear slightly left over tree-shaded grassy area with Crazy Fox ice cream kiosk and cycle-hire shop up to left. Now re-join cycleway and village of Edith Weston soon partially visible up to left. Follow cycleway as it wends round inlet with sailing harbour on far side. Bear left through gate and keep on cycleway behind sailing club. Through small metal gate to left of large one and turn right onto tarmac road (SP - *Lyndon Nature Reserve*). Pass caravan site on left and entry to Rutland Sailing Club on right.

(C) At end of tarmac bear left onto surfaced track and through small gate beside large metal one (SP - *Lyndon Nature Reserve*). Through small metal gate to right of large one and now views of the water to right from grassy banks. Keep on well surfaced cycleway as it curves around inlet and eventually passes fishermen's car park on right just before bending to left (SP - *Lyndon Nature Reserve*). Hambleton village just visible to right on hilly peninsula across water. Spire of Oakham Church just visible ahead right, well beyond head of reservoir. If conditions dry bear right off cycleway and head across meadow and into wood (if wet, keep on cycleway). Keep on path through wood and over small meadow into second wood. At end of this wood bear right to re-join cycleway. Hambleton Hall now visible over to right. Pass 9-hole golf course up to left. Distant Burley-on-the-Hill mansion now visible over to right.

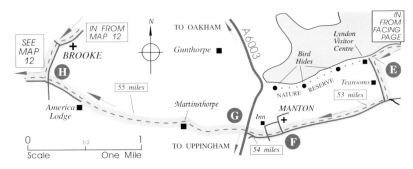

(D) Through small metal gate beside cattle-grid into Lyndon Nature Reserve area. Bushes on both sides are part of woodlands known as Gibbet Gorse. Pass metal gates to left and right (but only for the use of Reserve visitors). Pass Swan hide down to right (no entry from cycleway). Ignore bridleway signed to left.

(E) When reaching gate across track, turn left up narrow path between fences, and continue uphill on tarmac road *(unless you wish to visit the Lyndon Nature Reserve, when you would turn down right).* Eventually pass Page's Tearooms on right and soon over cattle-grid before turning right with care onto busier road (SP - *Manton*). Walk with care along reasonably wide verge soon passing nursery on right. After nearly a mile's boring walk along grass verge enter village of Manton.

(F) Go straight, not right, by minute bus shelter to right and telephone box to left (*no sign*). Go straight, not right, at next road junction (SP - *Oakham*) *(but turn down right if you wish to visit the Horse and Jockey Inn).* Now go carefully, probably crossing to left of road to keep to outside bend. Bear round to right keeping on main road.

(G) Soon cross very busy dual-carriageway A6003 with great care due to restricted vision both to left and right to go onto partially surfaced and signed bridleway. Good view of Gunthorpe Hall to right. Through double metal gates into large scrubby field and head towards double metal gates in wall-line ahead. Good view of Preston Hall and the spire of Preston Church across valley to left. Through gates and head slightly right towards solitary Old Hall Farm. Arrive at farmhouse and read plaque on east wall telling its story. *Now a substantial 17th-century ruin, it was first mentioned in 1199 as belonging to the de Montfort family. It was still being used as a farmhouse in 1949. The surrounding undulations are part of Martinsthorpe, a long deserted medieval village, while below, to its north, there was once a medieval manor house with a 17th-century garden.* Go round right-hand side of farmhouse and con-

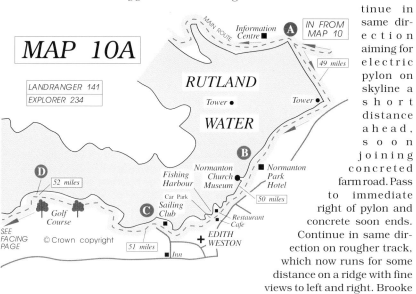

tinue in same direction aiming for electric pylon on skyline a short distance ahead, soon joining concreted farm road. Pass to immediate right of pylon and concrete soon ends. Continue in same direction on rougher track, which now runs for some distance on a ridge with fine views to left and right. Brooke village visible in valley ahead right. Pass roadway to America Lodge (farm) down to left. Go straight over X-rds onto public road (SP - *Braunston*) thereby re-joining main route at Map 12, <u>beyond</u> Point C, well to south of Brooke village (see page 34).

The Great Tower at Sykes Lane, Rutland Water (see page 29)

Continued from bottom of page 29

(A) Through metal gate at end of woodlands and head straight across track coming in from left and up grassy bank, keeping just to right of fence. *(If time allows, why not cross first stile to left and walk down to the shore here.)* There are fine views over Rutland Water from here, including the Limnological Tower, and the Secondary Draw-off Tower, which is almost opposite. Follow the fence as it climbs and bends to right and then veer right to join roadway just beyond car parks and refreshment building. *Toilets, Arboretum and Drought Garden are well up to right, the latter having been designed by much loved gardening expert, the late Geoff Hamilton.* Now bear left on roadway through the Barnsdale woodlands, first going downhill and then up again. *This follows the course of the old Oakham to Stamford Turnpike, one the old milestones of which is still to be seen on the left just beyond the ramp (see below).*

(B) Turn left beyond ramp and going downhill again *(but turn right if you wish to visit Barnsdale Hotel).* Through small metal gate just beyond The Lodge onto cycle track and keep on this, passing the modernistic wooden buildings of Barnsdale Country Club and Conference Centre up to right and old parkland with a few oak trees down to left. It is possible to go down to the shore here (but watch out for fly-casting anglers), although it would be easier to keep to the cycle track, passing to right of Lodge Inlet.

(C) Through metal gate and bear left onto tarmac path running parallel with the busy A606. *(We are joined here by the Viking Way, a long-distance path which comes down across Lincolnshire from the Humber Bridge and ends at Oakham.)* In its early stages our footpath path is well away from the road, but the nearer we get to Oakham, the nearer the path gets to the road. The next two miles will therefore be boring and rather noisy, but there is really no alternative if you wish to visit Oakham. There is also the compensation of splendid views across Rutland Water to the left, with the woods of Burley Park on right for much of the way.

(D) Pass two narrow belts of woodland on left, the second of which has a sheep dip beside it. At some distance beyond here, there is a good view back right of the magnificent early 18th-century mansion of Burley-on-the-Hill rising above the woods.

(E) Cross the busy A606 with great care not far beyond the sign for Egleton, at a crossing point with traffic island and beacons, and go down roadway to right. Where roadway turns left into sewage treatment works, go straight ahead into field, keeping to right of hedge. Over stile and keep to right of hedge. Eventually cross stile, through minute farmyard, bear left keeping to left of Dog Kennel Cottages, and then turn left onto track. Cross busy bypass road with great care and continue in same direction into the outskirts of Oakham along surfaced path through housing estate, crossing one estate road. Soon join footpath beside public road (*Woodland View*) with houses on both sides.

The 17th-century Buttercross, Oakham

(F) Turn left into busy Burley Road (B668), soon use controlled pedestrian crossing and continue in same direction. Cross road with care by roundabout and keep to immediate left of The Old House Tavern. Cross road immediately beyond tavern and onto tarmac path through park *(sign - Toilets)* passing old bandstand on right and castle earthworks over to left. Up narrower pathway passing in quick succession - Oakham's Old School, its churchyard and church on right, and its toilets and castle earthworks on left. Turn left at corner of churchyard, down short passage and into Market Square, passing entrance to Oakham School (over to right) and Oakham's Buttercross on right. Turn right at end of Market Square *(but turn left if you wish to visit the Castle Hall)*, and soon turn left into High Street, just beyond the Whipper In Hotel. Arrive at centre of Oakham with Library immediately ahead, and turn right into Mill Street. *(See Page 34 for further information on the delightful town of Oakham.)*

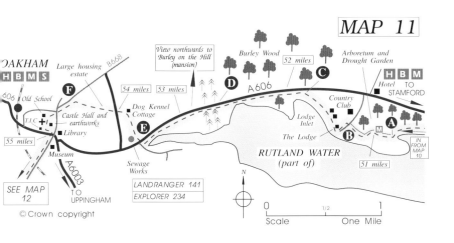

Do try to spare an hour or two to look round Oakham, England's smallest county town and the administrative centre of the County of Rutland. See especially the unique collection of outsize horseshoes in the 12th-century Castle Hall which is situated within the earthworks of the long vanished castle. See also the delightful 17th-century Buttercross and the slender spired parish church, the interior of which includes a fascinating series of carved arcade capitals. If time allows also try to visit the most interesting Rutland County Museum in Catmos Street.

Situated at the centre of the town, the Library stands at the southern end of the 140-mile Viking Way down from the Humber and at the western end of the 100-mile Hereward Way across from Thetford. Our own route from Oakham as far as Belton-in-Rutland also follows the same course as Rutland County Council's Leighfield Way.

(A) Continue walk from Oakham's main cross-roads turning right, down Mill Street (SP - *Brooke*). Mill Street soon becomes Brooke Road leading south-westwards out of Oakham. Over railway-crossing with care and turn left immediately beyond, continuing on Brooke Road (SP - *Brooke*). Leave Oakham by primary school on right and start to climb road up hill. *Views of Rutland Water over to left.*

(B) Turn left off road near top of hill just before small wood on left, and along track with hedges on both sides. Pleasant views down to right. Turn right, through gate where green road comes in from left and start going down into valley keeping to immediate right of hedge-line. Under power-line, through metal gate and second metal gate just beyond small mound on right. Continue down between two hedge-lines which get closer as we descend. Join smoother track by cottage on right and over old stone bridge crossing River Gwash. Pass Bridge Farm on right at entry to small village of Brooke, joining road and soon pass church on left. *Do not miss a visit to Brooke church, one of the most attractive churches on the whole route. It has a squat 13th-century tower and an exceptionally interesting and unspoilt interior including old stone floors, box pews, screens to both aisles and a fine 17th-century tomb.*

(C) Soon turn left at junction (SP - *Ridlington*) keeping on road out of valley with wide verges and young trees. Turn right at x-rds (SP - *Braunston*). *We are joined here by the Rutland Water South-Shore Alternative Route which comes in from the left*

- see Map 10A, page 31.) Keep on road past Shorne Hill and Hibbits Lodge on left.

(D) Turn left (SP - *Leigh Field Lodge*) onto still surfaced road and soon between stone gate pillars with Prior's Coppice over to right. Just before cottage on left pass entry on right to Prior's Coppice Nature Reserve. Go between second pair of stone gate pillars and onto broad, surfaced

Belton-in-Rutland Church

tree-lined bridleway (SP - *Leighfield Way*) passing farm buildings on left and starting to drop down to valley with fine views ahead.

(E) Bear left keeping on bridleway track to left of Leigh Lodge farm buildings and the fine old stone house of Leigh Lodge. Restored medieval fish ponds on both sides of track immediately before bridge crossing little River Chater. Climb out of valley on well surfaced track and eventually go between third pair of stone gate pillars by large barns on right.

(F) Turn left at junction of tracks just beyond barn and almost immediately turn right at second junction. Now start to drop down rough track into valley with hedge to right. Track improves as

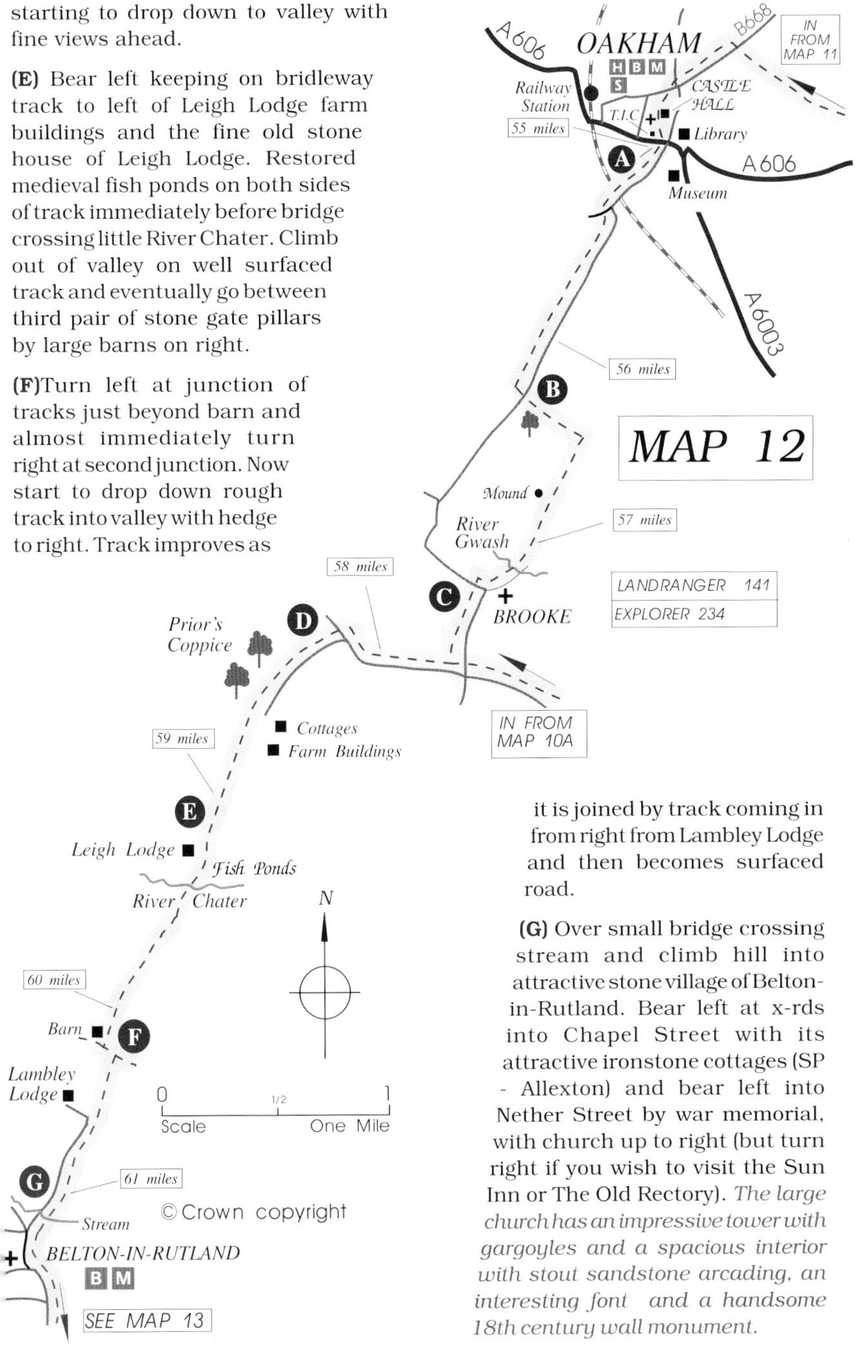

A 606
OAKHAM
B 668
IN FROM MAP 11
Railway Station
CASTLE HALL
T.I.C
55 miles
Library
A 606
A
Museum
A 6003
56 miles
B
MAP 12
Mound
River Gwash
57 miles
58 miles
C
BROOKE
LANDRANGER 141
EXPLORER 234
Prior's Coppice
D
Cottages
Farm Buildings
59 miles
IN FROM MAP 10A
E
Leigh Lodge
Fish Ponds
River Chater
N
60 miles
Barn
F
Lambley Lodge
0   1/2   1
Scale   One Mile
G
61 miles
© Crown copyright
Stream
BELTON-IN-RUTLAND
B M
SEE MAP 13

it is joined by track coming in from right from Lambley Lodge and then becomes surfaced road.

(G) Over small bridge crossing stream and climb hill into attractive stone village of Belton-in-Rutland. Bear left at x-rds into Chapel Street with its attractive ironstone cottages (SP - Allexton) and bear left into Nether Street by war memorial, with church up to right (but turn right if you wish to visit the Sun Inn or The Old Rectory). *The large church has an impressive tower with gargoyles and a spacious interior with stout sandstone arcading, an interesting font and a handsome 18th century wall monument.*

35

(A) Bear left down hill to leave Belton-in-Rutland. *(From Belton to Hallaton we share paths with the Leicestershire Round, a 100-mile circular walk around Leicestershire.)* Over the busy A47 with great care and continue on minor road to cross Eye Brook by Bridge House (once a mill). We now leave Rutland for Leicestershire and enter Allexton village. Go straight, not left at road junction, and up road with old rectory and church on left. *The church, in an overgrown churchyard, has a medieval tower, but most of the rest dates from the 19th century.* Bear left before reaching entrance gates ahead, keeping on road. Pass through pretty village green and at end go to right of last house on left *(Innisfree).* Up short, narrow path between overhanging bushes. At end of path, over fence, turn right and keep to immediate left of hedge-line until almost reaching gate at end of field. Good view of Allexton Hall down to right.

(B) Now bear half-left up hill to cut across corner of field towards electric pole. Over stile half-way up fence-line and head down across large field aiming just to left of house on horizon *(Allexton Lodge)* and, when they come into view, just to right of two trees. Over stile and small bridge and across second field, still aiming to left of Allexton Lodge. Go through gap in hedge and still aim for left-hand end of Allexton Lodge. On reaching stile in fence, do not cross it but note diversion of path along fence line to right. Now keep to right of Allexton Lodge.

(C) Turn left at end of fence and follow to right of fence up hill. Fine view back over valley of the Eye Brook to Belton-in-Rutland church tower. Now pass to right of Allexton Lodge and soon turn right to follow down to immediate right of hedge-line. At end of hedge go through gap between hedge and fence coming in from right and go straight across very small field heading slightly left towards small gate. Through gate and down field towards gap in hedge. Through gap and aim for right of Fearn Farm's buildings. Over stile and go left along farm track for a few yards to Fearn Farmhouse.

(D) Turn right, opposite farmhouse (SP - *Hallaton*) and through three metal gates, keeping to immediate left of hedge line. Over stile and then through metal gate. Go down field continuing to follow to left of hedge-line, with fine views ahead over rolling countryside to distant Northamptonshire skylines. Over double stile at bottom of field and head straight across large field on same line as hedge previously followed, aiming just to right of left-hand of two old railway bridges. Cross small bridge over stream and bear slightly left to left-hand of two railway bridges. Over this bridge crossing disused railway and through gap just beyond. Over fence and then keep to its immediate left for short distance. Through gap in left-hand corner of field and go diagonally across large field aiming for signpost soon visible at road junction. Over small bridge about two-thirds of the way across field, crossing small stream and soon go through large gate onto road at junction.

(E) Keep in same direction down road (SP - *Hallaton*) passing

Unusual Market Cross at Hallaton

sports pavilion on left and soon enter delightful village of Hallaton. Pass large duck-pond and Fox Inn on left. Well beyond Fox Inn bear right at junction (SP - *Cranoe*) passing attractive thatched cottages on right. Straight, not right, then next turn right into High Street. Keep down High Street and go straight onto path where street bends to right. Immediately pass old stone wellhead on right and then quaint little conical market cross and war memorial. *Do not miss the plaque on the wall just above, telling the story of the famous Bottle-Kicking Contest between*

IN FROM MAP 12

BELTON-IN-RUTLAND

B **M**

61 miles

A

LANDRANGER 141

EXPLORERS 233, 234

LEICESTER   UPPINGHAM

A47

Hall ■   Eye Brook

62 miles   ALLEXTON

MAP 13   **B**

To Sweethedges
Farm 1 mile

0   1/2   1

Scale   One Mile

C   ■ Allexton Lodge

OLD RAILWAY LINE

D

63 miles

■ Fearn Farm

64 miles

Hallaton and neighbouring Medbourne, an event that still takes place each Easter Monday. Cross road, with Bewicke Arms Inn to left (*with tea/gift shop next door*) and church well up to right. Go to right along road for few yards and then turn left through archway beneath house (watch for this carefully - it is easily missed). *But go straight ahead at this point if you wish to visit the church. This contains a wealth of beautiful features including a stone flagged floor and some unusually attractive 19th-century stained glass windows. Also do not miss the impressive Norman tympanum in the porch depicting St Michael slaying a dragon.*

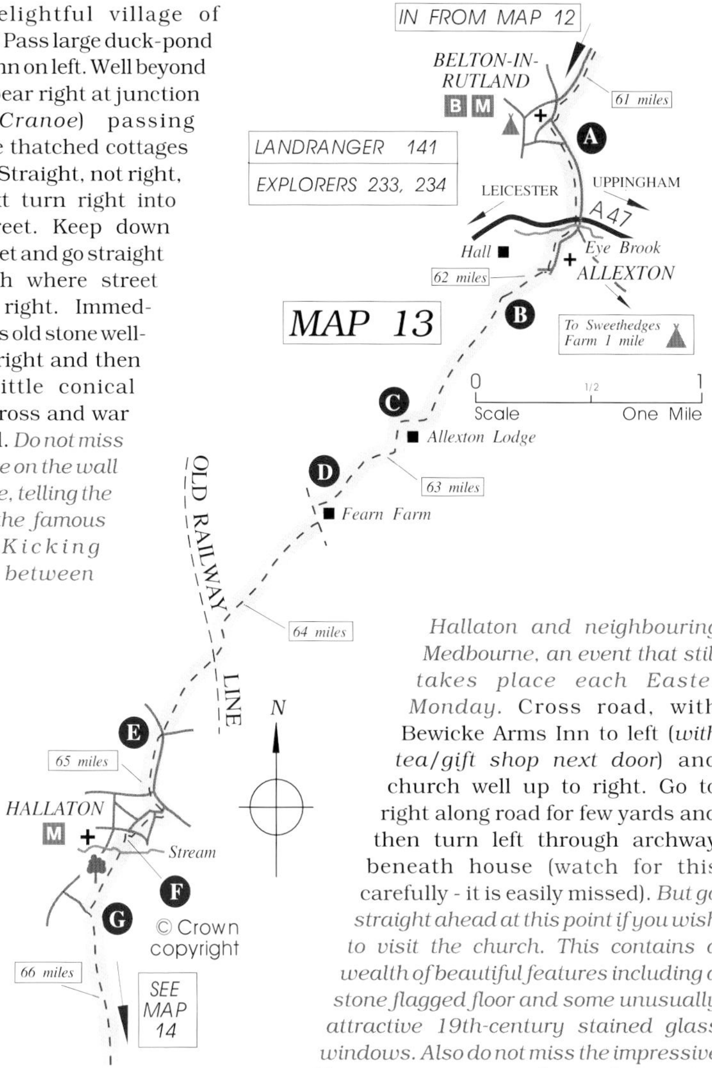

N

E

65 miles

HALLATON

M +

Stream

F

G   © Crown copyright

66 miles

SEE MAP 14

(F) Now back on route - go down narrow path beyond archway (*having now left the Leicestershire Round County Path*), over bridge crossing stream and over stile. Continue on same line up steep bank and across parkland passing end of wood on left. Good view back to Hallaton church and rectory.

(G) Through wooden gate at end of parkland and turn left onto track ignoring waymark sign on stile opposite. Go down track with hedges on both sides and attractive views ahead. Stubby spire of Slawston church visible over to right, with Slawston Hill to its left. At end of track, through wooden gate and head down left-hand side of two fields, with gate between them.

Springtime at Medbourne

(A) Through third wooden gate and turn left onto minor road. After 100 yards, where road bends to left, turn right onto roughly surfaced byway going upwards.

(B) After three-quarters-of-a-mile go over x-rds (SP - *Weston*). *(But turn left if you wish to divert to Medbourne for a night stop - 1 mile.) Medbourne is a charming village, complete with several pleasant 17th- and 18th-century houses, a stone-built inn and a three-arched medieval packhorse bridge across a stream just below its substantial church.*

(B) Back on main route - continue down pleasant road with high hedges on either side and good views ahead across broad Welland Valley. Just before going through gap in old railway embankment, cross course of Roman road which ran from Huntingdon to Leicester, but few signs of which remain.

(C) Soon pass bridleway signs on both sides of road. After almost half-a-mile go over small bridge crossing River Welland, which at this point is just to south of boundary between Leicestershire and Northamptonshire. For much of its length this river forms the boundary between these two counties. *Please note that throughout the course of its route through Northamptonshire the Macmillan Way will be waymarked by black and white signs provided by Northamptonshire County Council, rather than the normal green and white Macmillan waymarks.* Spire of Ashley church visible to south-east. Over hump in road by modern house on right, which probably replaced a level-crossing keeper's house, as we are crossing line of another old railway, signs of which are more apparent in cutting well over to right.

(D) Bear left at road junction (SP - *Ashley*) at entry to Weston-by-Welland with Wheel and Compass Inn on left. Soon bear right in centre of village onto B664 (SP - *Market Harborough*). *The village has a few pleasant ironstone houses and a church which was largely rebuilt in the 19th century.* Pass telephone box on right.

(E) Cross road with care just beyond first bend on B664 and through gate opposite stone house and into field. Go upwards, straight across field, through gate and straight across next field to reach small fenced gap near electric pole. Over fenced gap in hedge and head upwards, keeping to immediate right of hedge with minute wind turbine and at end of hedge turn left through large metal gate. Keep hedge on immediate right, then through gate. Turn right through second gate and follow hedge keeping to its immediate left.

(F) At end of hedge turn left near small building and small pond and follow track to left of hedge-line. Under high-voltage power-line, fine views to left of rolling Leicestershire country beyond Welland Valley. Through metal gate and keep hedge on immediate right. Through another metal gate and bear slightly to right following bending hedge-line. Good open, upland country here, as we pass small pond on right.

(G) Arrive at impressively tall, six-way concrete marker post. *We are joined here by the Midshires Way - a 225-mile long-distance path and bridleway linking the Trans-Pennine Trail near Stockport with the Ridgeway in Buckinghamshire. At times the 'Walkers Route' diverges from the 'Riders Route', but our route is common with the 'Walkers Route' as far as Maidwell - see* *page 43.)* Beyond six-way post keep in same direction with hedge-line on right aiming at spire of Brampton Ash church, which is about one-and-a-half miles to south-east. At end of field turn right through small gate and head down side of field with hedge to left. Good views across valley to Brampton Ash church, complemented by impressive line of mature ash trees in hedge to left of path. Through gate and continue on same line, but when ground starts to drop down ahead, turn left through small gate. Head almost due south down hill with hedge on immediate right, now aiming to right of Brampton Ash church.

(H) Now on edge of very large field in valley and keep to immediate left of hedge where it takes slight bend to right. Turn left at far corner of field and after about 40 yards, turn right through gate. Go slightly uphill, straight across small field to another gate. Turn left onto track after going through gate, keeping hedge on left *(watch for holes in path - badgers abound here !)* and follow around field by bearing right in next two half corners. Just beyond point where hedge comes in from left, turn left through gate and head diagonally across small field to cross stile to arrive at busy A427 by traffic layby.

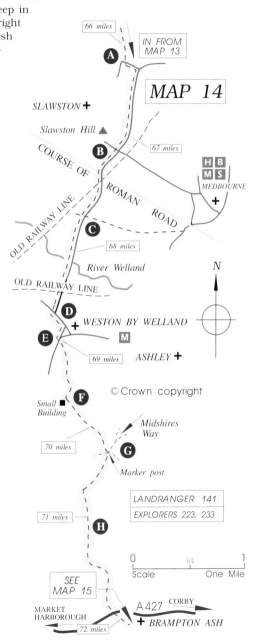

66 miles

IN FROM MAP 13

MAP 14

SLAWSTON ✝

Slawston Hill ▲

COURSE OF

67 miles

H B
M S
MEDBOURNE
✝

ROMAN ROAD

OLD RAILWAY LINE

68 miles

River Welland

OLD RAILWAY LINE

N

WESTON BY WELLAND
✝
M

69 miles   ASHLEY ✝

© Crown copyright

Small ■
Building

Midshires Way

70 miles

Marker post

LANDRANGER 141
EXPLORERS 223, 233

71 miles

0   1/2   1
Scale   One Mile

SEE MAP 15

MARKET HARBOROUGH

A 427   CORBY
✝ BRAMPTON ASH

72 miles

(A) Cross A427 with great care and through kissing gate slightly to left. Now head diagonally left across field to immediate right of line of trees. Through kissing gate and head diagonally across next field aiming for right-hand end of tall Leylandii hedge. Good view of Brampton Ash church over to left. Through fence-line obliquely and pass end of Leylandii hedge. Through two kissing gates and turn right onto road *(But turn left and left again if you wish to visit church (usually locked). This is an impressive building with elegant broach spire, many lovely early-19th-century gravestones in its churchyard and two porches, both with tall doorways within.* Now back on main route and drop down into valley.

(B) Soon turn left off road through metal gate. Go to immediate right of attractive mellow-brick barns known as Red Hovel and through metal gate just beyond. Go quietly up field following to immediate left of hedge-line until reaching corner of Brampton Wood on left. Before turning right, look ahead, as deer from neighbouring woods often graze on the grass track visible from here.

(C) At this corner of wood turn right over small stone bridge (*not very apparent*) to join the Jurassic Way. *The Jurassic Way is a Northamptonshire County Path, running for 88 miles between Stamford in Lincolnshire and Banbury in Oxfordshire. We not only follow it between here and Great Oxendon, but will also join it again between Eydon and Chipping Warden.* Over stile to go diagonally left across narrow belt of plantation and cross stile on its far side. Now aim for left-hand end of Hermitage Wood, beyond the brow. Join track running parallel with the left-hand (southern) edge of Hermitage Wood noting a mass of bluebells if you come here in May (Do not enter wood, which is private). Through several gates and eventually turn left onto road.

(D) Soon turn right on to what may already be the old A6 road (SP - *Market Harborough*), go along north side of this before turning left to cross the new A6 by-pass with very great care. (See Update Sheet for latest information on these works.) Head diagonally right across field beyond aiming for mast on distant horizon (although this is not always visible) and once over first brow, head for gate.

Through this metal gate and go straight downhill to stile immediately ahead. Through gate at end of hedge and drop down, going diagonally right and aiming for Park Hill Farm's buildings. Over stile well to right of gate close to dutch barn and leave farmyard. Go straight across road and over stile into field. Go diagonally left, aiming for white-painted stile. Over stile, under railway embankment and over second stile. Now turn right and go parallel with railway for short distance before bearing left to cross bridge over stream. Soon cross another bridge, turn left and follow to immediate right of hedge. Leave hedge where it turns left and head across field aiming to left of barns.

(E) Over double stile and turn right onto road. *Earthworks of Braybrooke Castle visible to right. Medieval home of the Latimer family and later, in Tudor times, of the Griffins, it must have once been an impressive building, but nothing now remains above ground.* Bear left

Bridge over the Jordan, Braybrooke

40

just beyond entry to Braybrooke and down School Lane (SP - *Arthingworth*). Keep straight along School Lane and turn right onto Griffin Road by Swan Inn (SP - *Market Harborough*). Pass village hall, cross River Jordan and then turn left into Newland Street by Baptist Chapel. *But turn right if you wish to visit the largely 13th-century church. This has a slender broach spire and a number of interesting monuments including one of Sir Thomas Latimer carved out of a single piece of oak. This local knight left money in his will for the completion of the three-arched bridge, which still spans the little River Jordan, just to the south-east of the church.* Back on main route - having turned left into Newland Street, follow road soon changing to dirt-surfaced track. Follow this, ignoring waymark to left, under high-voltage power-line and cross small bridge over River Jordan.

(**F**) Follow track as it bears sharply to left by stables on right. *(But bear slightly right off track, and onto footpath if you wish to link on to the Brampton Valley Way (see page 42) to go north into Market Harborough for overnight accommodation - two-and-a-half miles. It would be possible to walk south next morning, down Brampton Valley Way (see below) to re-join main route by tunnel entrance near Great Oxendon, a further two-and-a-half miles).* Back on main route - ascend small hill and look back for rewarding views north-eastwards across the Jordan valley to Braybrooke.

(**G**) About a quarter-of-a-mile beyond hill and about 50 yards before second hedge converges from left, turn right by bench, off track onto path. Follow path across stile heading towards buildings on next hill *(Waterloo Lodge).* Down path into valley, crossing one stile, a pond on left and then another stile, before climbing directly up other side towards buildings. Cross stile, go up between fence on left and hedge on right and on brow of hill, cross yet another stile (passing to right of *Waterloo Lodge* - a series of converted farm buildings). Follow fence on immediate left, and cross stile just beyond metal gate in fence to left.

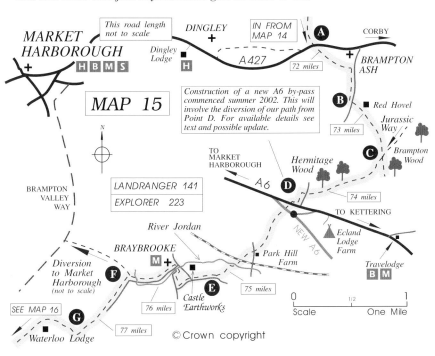

© Crown copyright

41

(A) Bear left to follow clear-cut path diagonally across grass and through spinney of young trees. Cross stile. Keep in same line across next field to go over double-stile well to left of large ash tree. Keep in same line across next field, first aiming well to left of two large trees in facing hedge and once over slight brow, head for double-stile. Over this double-stile, go in same line, diagonally across next roller-coaster field, aiming for stile on edge of woodlands. Good view of Great Oxendon church over to right. In winter, ventilation shaft of railway tunnel just visible through hedge to left.

(B) Over stile, follow muddy path down through scrubby woodland and pass over twin tunnels of disused railway line (not usually visible from this path). At far edge of woodland, branch right to

The Brampton Valley Way

go along bank and then down to disused railway line. *(Now leaving the Jurassic Way.) (But branch left and go over fields if you wish to divert to Great Oxendon for overnight stop - about 250 yards).* Now back to main route, having followed path down to where it converges with bed of disused railway line. Turn sharp right just before brick bridge and go back (southwards) along line. *This is the Brampton Valley Way, which we shall be following for 4 miles. This is a 14-mile linear park based on a former railway line between Market Harborough and Northampton, the embankments and cuttings of which are rich with wildflowers. Some walkers may find this stretch rather bland, but we feel that it provides a pleasant contrast with some of the harder cross-farmland sections.* Now head southwards, taking left fork which is more heavily used. Enter left-hand (east) railway tunnel, which is over 450 yards long and a fine example of Victorian civil engineering. The exit can always be seen as the tunnel is straight, but a torch would certainly be useful, especially for spotting possible puddles.

(C) Follow Brampton Valley Way southwards beyond tunnel. Pass old level-crossing which allows access on right to A508. Soon cross viaduct over small stream and about half-a-mile beyond, pass over small underbridge where footpath between Arthingworth and A508 crosses. Continue down Brampton Valley Way and cross infant River Ise, tributary of River Nene, which it joins at Wellingborough.

(D) Pass large depot, car park and picnic area on left before crossing minor road from Arthingworth. After some distance fork slightly left beyond picnic table to take higher of two tracks into left-hand (east) tunnel (520 yards). Beyond tunnel go under busy A14 road and again continue southwards on

17th-century gateway at Maidwell

Brampton Valley Way. Cross line of bridleway between Harrington and Maidwell, pass Draughton Car Park and Picnic Area on left where we cross Maidwell to Draughton road.

(E) Soon turn right over stile leaving Brampton Way and Midshires Way near old metal footbridge (SP - *Maidwell Village*). Down across narrow field and over bridge with two stiles crossing brook. Head up field keeping to immediate left of hedge. At top of rise veer left and aim for small gate. Through small gate at entry to Maidwell and join road by church on left and school on right. *The squat towered church is largely 13th and 14th century and contains a colourful 17th-century monument to Lady Gorges and her husband, Lord Dundalk.* Keep on road into centre of Maidwell passing elegant 17th-century gateway on right. This used to stand at the entrance to Maidwell Hall's kitchen garden and was moved a few yards to its present site in 1914.

(F) Cross busy A508 with great care (but turn right if you wish to visit Stag's Head - just visible beside A508). Bear round slightly to left on surfaced road opposite to one from which we have just crossed (SP - *Dale Farm*) (ignoring footpath sign). Go along surfaced road with fine views ahead as road drops down. Pass sign on left indicating 'Dale Farm Conservation Area' - pleasant piece of woodland. Bear left at road junction ignoring both bridleway and footpath signs. Good views ahead as country opens out.

(G) Pass Blueberry Lodge barns and farmhouse on right, with track soon becoming less well surfaced and more interesting, first bordered by hedges and then with large open grass fields to right and then left.

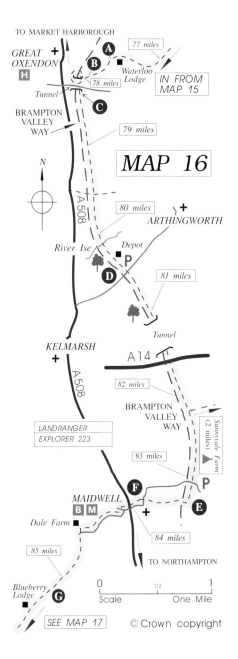

(A) Track becomes better surfaced again and soon pass wood on right. Through gateway onto surfaced road with parkland on right. Trees on right obscure views of park, but eventually there is a distant glimpse of south-east front of elegant, early 18th-century Cottesbrooke Hall up avenue of young trees over to right. This may possibly have been the inspiration for Jane Austen's *Mansfield Park*.

(B) Over road beyond large farm buildings on left, going slightly to left, through large wooden gate. *But turn right and walk along road if you wish to visit delightful Cottesbrooke village - the unspoilt Georgian interior of the church and elegant entrance gates to Cottesbrooke Hall making this well worthwhile.* Back on main route - having gone through large wooden gate, head for far right-hand corner of field. Over small stile to right of double gates, then go straight across field to large double gates and towards right-hand end of Creaton village which is visible on skyline ahead. Over small stile to right of double gates, over bridge crossing stream and immediately turn left and through more double gates. Follow along to immediate right of hedge with stream just to its left. Through wide gap at next hedge-line across path and bend slightly round to left near end of field.

(C) Through gap in hedge and turn right, going up hill to immediate left of hedge-line. Follow this line as far as road and bear left to soon enter pretty ironstone and brick village of Creaton. Bear right at first road junction (SP - *Welford*) and soon bear left at next road junction to climb up High Street. Bear left onto wider road beyond Post Office Stores on right, with church on left. Attractive village green well over to right. Leave Creaton by road up past church. Turn right with care onto busy A5199 (SP - *Leicester*) and almost immediately cross road to go through metal gate. Follow well surfaced track down hill, going over stile by wooden gate and through area with wooden stables on right. Through gate beyond stable yard and another gate. Over double-stile and go diagonally half-right to cross footbridge.

(D) Bear right to cross small field to stile in right-hand corner. Cross stile, continue up field keeping to immediate left of hedge, climbing out of valley and through gap in hedge at end of field. Keep up hill along same line as previously. Pleasant view of Hollowell village and church over to right. Now go to immediate left of re-started hedge. At end of this long field go over stile, down hill and veer right following to immediate left of curving hedge-line before starting to climb again. Pastures Farm visible over to right. Continue up hill, through large gap in fragmentary hedge-line coming in from left. Over stile and footbridge in hedge and bear round to right following to left of hedge, soon passing small clump of trees on right before turning left onto road.

(E) Walk down road and bear half-left at five-way x-rds at entry to Teeton (SP - *Spratton*) (but bear left if you wish to visit Teeton, although no items of real interest here, apart from phone box). Walk with care, road verges are very narrow and traffic can be fast.

(F) Turn right at x-rds on bend (SP - *Holdenby*) and keep on road dropping gently down into valley, past old mill house on right and start

Our path near Creaton

to climb other side. At entrance to Holdenby North Lodge, by house on right, cross road and over stile by gate, leaving road to head across field diagonally half right going over stile in fence. Soon aim for stile by large metal gate in second fence (not immediately visible). Over stile by water trough and veer slightly left to pass between two clumps of trees. Over stile at far end of field and continue in same direction to aim for left-hand end of Holdenby woodlands. Over stile and aim for stone house (once a lodge).

(G) Through metal gate and over road with care to enter Holdenby village on surfaced road with wide grass verges. *But go to right along road before turning left, if you wish to visit Holdenby House Gardens and Falconry Centre. The original Holdenby House was built by Elizabeth I's*

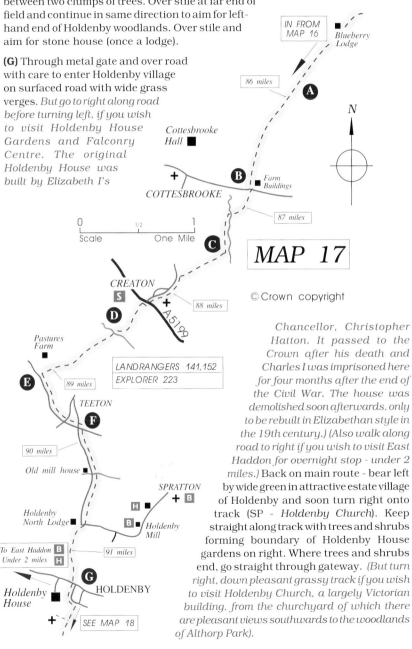

IN FROM MAP 16

Blueberry Lodge

86 miles

A

N

Cottesbrooke Hall ■

B

Farm Buildings

COTTESBROOKE

87 miles

0   1/2   1
Scale   One Mile

C

MAP 17

© Crown copyright

CREATON

S

88 miles

D

A5199

Pastures Farm ■

LANDRANGERS 141,152
EXPLORER 223

E

89 miles

TEETON

F

90 miles

Old mill house ■

SPRATTON

H ■   + B

Holdenby North Lodge ■

B ■ Holdenby Mill

To East Haddon B
Under 2 miles H

91 miles

G HOLDENBY

Holdenby House

+ SEE MAP 18

Chancellor, Christopher Hatton. It passed to the Crown after his death and Charles I was imprisoned here for four months after the end of the Civil War. The house was demolished soon afterwards, only to be rebuilt in Elizabethan style in the 19th century.) (Also walk along road to right if you wish to visit East Haddon for overnight stop - under 2 miles.) Back on main route - bear left by wide green in attractive estate village of Holdenby and soon turn right onto track (SP - *Holdenby Church*). Keep straight along track with trees and shrubs forming boundary of Holdenby House gardens on right. Where trees and shrubs end, go straight through gateway. *(But turn right, down pleasant grassy track if you wish to visit Holdenby Church, a largely Victorian building, from the churchyard of which there are pleasant views southwards to the woodlands of Althorp Park).*

(A) Back on main route - having gone through gateway beyond turn to Holdenby church, continue in same direction down track across field with mound to right. Through gateway at bottom of field and keep in same direction with hedge on immediate left. Then turn right, following cross-hedge now on left and follow long track. Good views back to Holdenby House, above the church. Through gap in hedge at end of field and head straight across field on rough track aiming just to right of modern barns. Great Brington church visible on skyline ahead left, with woodlands to its left being part of Althorp Park. Still heading to right of barns.

(B) Through small gate and turn left near barns onto busy A428 and immediately cross with great care to utilise wide verge on far side. Beyond cottages on right go onto path beneath railway bridge and then turn right onto minor road (SP - *Great Brington*). (Regrettably we shall follow this road into Great Brington, but there is no alternative.) As our road bends slightly to right it is joined by the impressive stone wall of Althorp Park and we follow this for some distance up hill. *The splendid 17th- and 18th-century mansion of Althorp, the home of Earl Spencer, is hidden in its great park, well to our left.*

(C) Straight, not left near Great Brington entry sign (*possibly passing gates on road to left*), and then straight not right, with church up to left. *This is a fine building with a lovely old roof to its nave and many other interesting features. Its North Chapel has a splendid series of Spencer tombs, and although enclosed by spiked iron railings, these monuments are well worth looking at. The adjoining rectory, with its polygonal tower, has a rather Tudor flavour, but is in fact, an early 19th-century building. The village beyond is a pleasant mixture of stone, brick and some thatch, with many estate-built houses and cottages.* Beyond church, keep straight down village street, with war memorial on left and small triangular green on right, complete with large horse-chestnut tree and telephone box just behind it. Pass on right, Post Office and pleasant Fox and Hounds Inn (also called 'The Althorp Coaching Inn'). Bear round to right just beyond and leave village on footpath beside minor road.

(D) At about a quarter-of-a-mile beyond village, where road starts to bend to left, turn right at second of two footpaths, through kissing gate and go diagonally across field following sign's direction. Over bridge and go diagonally right across field following well defined path. Through kissing gate at top of field and change direction slightly left, initially aiming for Little Brington church spire and then aiming for white disc marker just to right of small tin-roofed shed. Through kissing gate and up narrow field keeping to right-hand edge. Through kissing gate and turn right onto road in Little Brington. (But turn left if you wish to visit village shop.) *This village has stone buildings, some of which are Althorp estate houses. Its Victorian church was demolished some years ago and all that remains is a handsome tower with broach spire - a rather sad landmark well away from the village.* Pass The Old Saracen's Head Inn on right keeping on road.

(E) Turn left at small X-rds roads before end of village and leave it on road passing last house on left (*Stoneacre*), with stables just beyond. Soon turn left onto busier road, *which follows the course of a Roman road which ran from a settlement at Duston near Northampton to link with the Watling Street near Whilton.* After about 100 yards turn right at end of large layby down well-defined track with tall hedge on its left. Now descending into broad Nene valley with good views of hill country beyond. Keep on track through gaps in two successive cross-hedges with hedge still to our left. Targets of rifle range just visible below wood to left. Now turn left, through wooden gate at end of track and immediately turn right to follow hedge to immediate right.

(F) Ignore metal gate in hedge ahead and turn right before corner of field to cross stile and sleeper bridge. Cross field heading towards barns ahead and over stile and sleeper bridge in second corner. Bear left beyond stile and follow hedge-line to immediate left. Through low metal gate and turn right aiming for buildings of Vicarage Farm, but almost immediately, turn left over sleeper bridge and stile. Through narrow, young plantation and over second stile. Head straight across field keeping in same direction as previously, aiming to immediate right of line of trees along cross-hedge ahead.

(G) Over stile, pass between two narrow pools with signs of wildfowl and over second stile. Keep straight across field in same direction as previously, aiming for double gates, but go over two closely spaced stiles in hedge about 10 yards to right of gates. Go diagonally across field veering slightly to right of previous direction and aiming for gap in hedge. Through gate just to right of re-entrant corner of field. Now head diagonally across small field with pronounced dip. Over small stile half-way along opposite fence and go diagonally across field, now aiming just to left of closest electric pylon, to cross double-stile with bridge between, and small pools to left and right. Up bank and

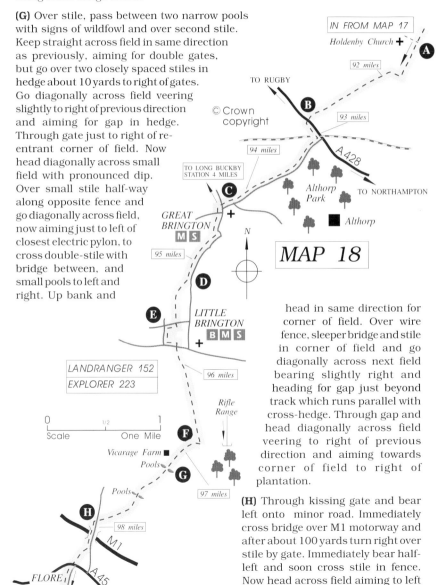

IN FROM MAP 17

Holdenby Church ✝

A

92 miles

TO RUGBY

B

93 miles

© Crown copyright

A428

94 miles

Althorp Park

TO NORTHAMPTON

TO LONG BUCKBY STATION 4 MILES

C

■ Althorp

GREAT BRINGTON ✝
M **S**

N

MAP 18

95 miles

D

E

LITTLE BRINGTON
B **M** **S**
✝

LANDRANGER 152
EXPLORER 223

96 miles

Rifle Range

0   1/2   1
Scale   One Mile

F

Vicarage Farm ■
Pools

G

97 miles

Pools

H

98 miles

M1

FLORE
H **M**
✝

A45

SEE MAP 19

head in same direction for corner of field. Over wire fence, sleeper bridge and stile in corner of field and go diagonally across next field bearing slightly right and heading for gap just beyond track which runs parallel with cross-hedge. Through gap and head diagonally across field veering to right of previous direction and aiming towards corner of field to right of plantation.

(H) Through kissing gate and bear left onto minor road. Immediately cross bridge over M1 motorway and after about 100 yards turn right over stile by gate. Immediately bear half-left and soon cross stile in fence. Now head across field aiming to left of garage building at entry to Flore.

Chapter 4 Flore - Warmington   22 Miles

(A) Over stile by garage forecourt at entry to Flore and cross often busy A45 with very great care (if busy, use controlled pedestrian crossing along to right). Go down Sutton Street, just to right of White Hart Inn. *Flore is a stone and thatch village, pleasantly quiet once away from the A45.* Telephone box soon on left. On edge of village, turn right at end of Sutton Street onto slightly busier road. Soon turn right at end of Nether Lane, into Spring Lane and almost immediately turn left to pass Brodie Lodge Playing Field notice. *Our path is now common with the Nene Way, a Northamptonshire County Path, stretching 70 miles between Wansford-in-England in Cambridgeshire and Badby, near Daventry. We shall share paths until reaching bridge over Grand Union Canal at Weedon Bec.* Up path with high hedges on either side, turn left by primary school, down road called *The Avenue* and into churchyard. *Looking out over the Nene valley from its tree-lined churchyard, the largely 13th- and 14th-century church has a stout tower and an interior with fine arcading and a medieval screen.* Go straight down churchyard, keeping well to left of church. Through kissing gate and go diagonally across large field following well defined path (much used by dog-walkers - tread carefully!).

(B) Over bridge crossing River Nene and follow well defined path bearing slightly to left. Over smaller bridge crossing minute stream and turn right keeping ditch and hedge on immediate right, aiming for right of garage (probably still white painted) at Weedon Bec. Cross the still busy A5 with great care. *(But turn left and walk with care up left-hand side of A5 if you wish to visit Narrowboat Inn - pub, motel and restaurant - but safer to go a little further along main route and then walk back along canal towpath.) The A5 follows the course of Watling Street - the road built by the Romans to link their channel ports to London and the great legionary fortress at Chester. It is interesting to note that this busy transport corridor, first opened up by the Romans, now carries not only the A5, but also the Grand Union Canal, the busy railway line beside it and the M1 motorway not far away.* Having drawn breath on far side of A5, take minor road (SP - *Lower Weedon*) and almost immediately bear left onto well surfaced track. Soon go straight, not left (left-hand track is to sewage works only) and start to gently climb up from Nene valley. Over bridge crossing Grand Union Canal. *A link here between the Macmillan Way and the Grand Union Canal Walk - a 140-mile long-distance path between London and Birmingham. The canal itself runs from Birmingham to the tidal River Thames at Brentford and has its origins in the closing years of the 18th century. The Nene Way turns right here and also uses the canal towpath for a short distance. (Use towpath to walk left to Narrowboat Inn more safely than along A5 (see above), or to walk right to Weedon with its several hotels, pubs and restaurants).*

(C) Go over busy railway line which runs parallel with canal here. Over stile beside metal gate and continue on track up hill. Church Stowe church tower soon visible

well over to left beyond valley. Turn sharp left off track immediately in front of metal gate and follow down edge of field with hedge on immediate right. At bottom of field go over concrete bridge and turn half-right to go up hill through very large field in general direction of Stowe church tower. *Loose oolitic (Cotswold) stone much in evidence in this field.* Over stile and continue in same direction up small, steeper field. Note

Well cleared path beyond Flore Church

fine views back over the Nene valley. Over another stile and cross bushy field with church up to left, and through small gate at entry to Church Stowe.

(D) Turn right onto road (but turn left if you wish to visit church). *Church and village are poised on a steep slope looking northwards over the busy and already remote Nene Valley. The church has a slender, largely Saxon tower and a small Norman north doorway. Within will be found two exceptionally fine monuments, a 13th-century armoured knight in Purbeck marble, Sir Gerard de L'Isle, and a beautifully carved Lady Elizabeth Carey, by the well-known 17th-century sculptor, Nicholas Stone. There is also a good wall monument to Doctor Thomas Turner, President of Corpus Christi College, Oxford, who died in 1714.* Continue on road through Church Stowe village, with minute Post Office on left and telephone box on right. Keep straight out of village on road, soon ignoring footpath sign to left and pass bench on left. Ignore second footpath sign to left, and eventually pass entry to *The Larches* bungalow on right.

(E) Soon bear right by small triangular green onto slightly busier road (SP - *Farthingstone*). Pass Stowe Heights Farm on right, entry to *Stowe Lodge* on left and Lodge Plantation on left just beyond. Beyond house on right, views start to open up ahead as road begins to drop slightly. Entry to wood known as Ramsden Corner Plantation on right. Almost immediately after this gateway, go through easily missed gap in hedge on opposite (left) side of road and immediately turn right to climb fence. Head diagonally across field following direction of fingerpost and soon aiming for stile in cross-hedge. Over stile and continue in same direction across narrow field to stile in hedge. Over stile and veer slightly left to follow path across field.

(F) Bear left to follow remains of wall-line for about 100 yards and then veer right aiming for left-hand end of narrow conifer plantation in valley. Drop down across this large field and over bridge to immediate left of conifer plantation. Continue in same direction aiming for slight gap in hedge below right-hand end of modern barn visible beyond opposite side of road. Through gap in hedge by waymark post, bear left onto road and up hill soon passing Farthingstone entry sign.

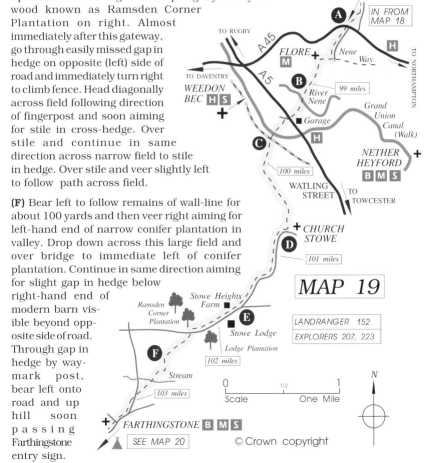

SEE MAP 20

© Crown copyright

49

Canons Ashby House

(A) Bear right at entry to Farthingstone keeping on road (SP - Everdon) and (hopefully) pass Post Office Stores and telephone box on left *(Stock up here - shops on route ahead are very thin on the ground). Pass gate in wall on left which is the entrance to a poignant garden of remembrance - a good place to stop awhile.* Turn left by Kings Arms Inn on right and church ahead (SP - *Maidford*). *Farthingstone is a pleasant village with ironstone houses and cottages. The attractive church, also of ironstone, has a 13th-century tower and sits comfortably in its churchyard across the road from the neo-Tudor inn.* Continue out of Farthingstone village, past entrances on left to *Littlecourt Yard* and *Little Court*, where road bends round to left.

(B) Soon, after telegraph pole on right, turn half-right through metal gate. Ignore obvious track along right-hand boundary of field and follow path diagonally left across field towards two ash trees in opposite corner. Go through large gap in hedge in corner of field into next field. Pass close to oak tree on right before turning slightly left towards small gap in hedge ahead. Through this gap, turn half-right to follow distinct path across field towards corner to left of two large oak trees. *Note radio beacon possibly visible up to left - a strange, low building looking almost 'extra-terrestrial'.* At corner go straight ahead through gap in hedge and over metal gate. Now follow left-hand hedge to gate visible in corner of field. Through metal gate and go straight ahead following right-hand hedge. Through three more gates to reach a metal gate at road.

(C) Over stile beside gate, turn right onto road and after 75 yards turn left onto byway track. Continue along byway past Tunningham Farm to reach T-junction with minor road.

(D) Turn left onto this road and go slightly up hill. Go straight, not left at road junction (SP - *Preston Capes*).

(E) After 500 yards, turn left where road comes in from right to go through small gate (SP - *Byway*). Go along track, known as Oxford Lane, with hedge to right and open field to left. Soon passing wood on right known as Ashby Gorse.

(F) After small wood on left, cross concrete farm road to continue on grassy track with hedge and trees on right. Immediately after cross-hedge comes in from right, turn right to go over stile. Tower of Canons Ashby church now visible

Quiet lane beyond Moreton Pinkney

ahead. Go diagonally left across field aiming for hedge corner to right of clump of trees in middle distance and to right of church tower. A hedge and gate soon come into view. Through gate and continue in same direction across large field. Follow line that passes close to hedge-corner sighted earlier and from there to right of single large ash tree. Through metal gate well to right of ash tree. Now go diagonally across park-like field with several mature trees, aiming for church tower with Canons Ashby House just to its right.

(G) Over stile opposite Canons Ashby House, cross road and go down gravel path to immediate left of the house - this path is not a right-of-way, but is kindly permitted by the National Trust. *Home of the Dryden family since the 16th century, Canons Ashby is now owned by the National Trust and well worth visiting. Having escaped the attentions of 19th-century improvers, it is full of atmosphere and looks out over recently restored formal gardens to extensive parklands beyond. The poet John Dryden often visited his uncle here.* Follow gravel path through paddock *(but turn left if you wish to visit the church, which, with its massive tower, is the surviving west end of a 200-ft long church built by Black Augustinian Canons who had a priory here and, like the house, should not be overlooked.* Go through car park, bear left onto minor road and almost immediately turn right at road

junction (SP - Banbury) and walk down road with great care.

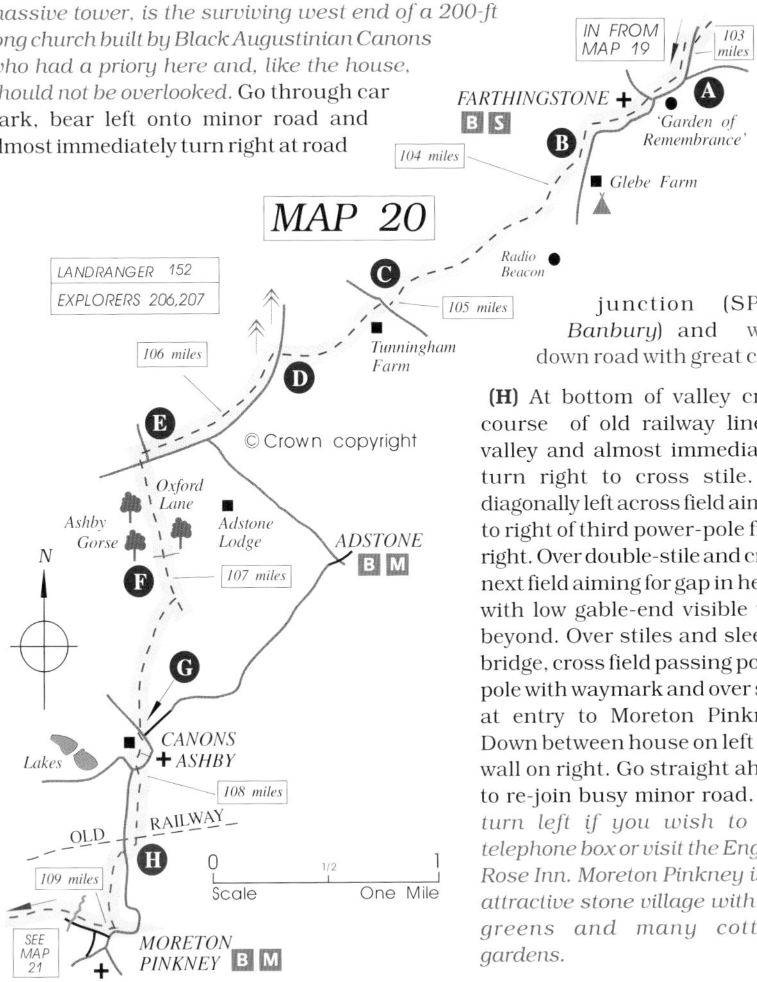

(H) At bottom of valley cross course of old railway line in valley and almost immediately turn right to cross stile. Go diagonally left across field aiming to right of third power-pole from right. Over double-stile and cross next field aiming for gap in hedge with low gable-end visible well beyond. Over stiles and sleeper bridge, cross field passing power pole with waymark and over stile at entry to Moreton Pinkney. Down between house on left and wall on right. Go straight ahead to re-join busy minor road. *But turn left if you wish to use telephone box or visit the English Rose Inn. Moreton Pinkney is an attractive stone village with two greens and many cottage gardens.*

MAP 20

IN FROM MAP 19

103 miles

FARTHINGSTONE
B S

A

'Garden of Remembrance'

B

104 miles

Glebe Farm

LANDRANGER 152

EXPLORERS 206,207

106 miles

Radio Beacon

C

105 miles

Tunningham Farm

D

E

© Crown copyright

Oxford Lane

Ashby Gorse

Adstone Lodge

ADSTONE
B M

F

107 miles

N

G

Lakes

CANONS ASHBY

108 miles

OLD RAILWAY

109 miles

H

0   1/2   1

Scale   One Mile

SEE MAP 21

MORETON PINKNEY
B M

51

(A) In Moreton Pinkney, soon turn right into Brook Street just before reaching Victorian turreted archway. Go straight, not left, at small road junction and leave village by going over footbridge to right of ford. Immediately go straight, not left, and pass seat on right (this will confirm that you are on the right track and also provide an excuse for a rest). Now follow partly surfaced, hedge-lined track, bordered by trees in places. After half-a-mile go through metal gate, follow track on right-hand edge of field , and through second metal gate onto track with hedges again on both sides. Track soon bends to right with tall pine trees sheltering sad remains of long-vanished railway line running parallel on left - *this was the Great Central Railway - a line that never paid its way.*

(B) Soon turn left onto road to go over bridge crossing course of railway and almost immediately, where road bends to left, bear right up track which is a bridleway. Track soon starts to go downwards and becomes narrower path with hedge to left and fence to right. Through underbridge beneath embankment of another disused railway and bear left before going through thick cross-hedge. Keep on left-hand edge of field with broad grassy headland and then turn right at cross hedge to follow on right-hand edge of next field, also with grassy headland.

(C) Bear left at corner of field and follow right-hand edge with parallel stream bordered by rough grass and trees not far below to right. At bottom of field where hedge and trees come in from left, go to right, through gate, over bridge crossing stream and through second gate. Follow to right of line of trees bordering tributary stream and to left of power-line. Through gap in cross-hedge coming in from right and soon turn left onto surfaced track with hedge to left, climbing up to Eydon.

(D) Turn left onto road at entry to Eydon and immediately bear right up School Lane by entrance to Eydon Hall on left. *Here is a village green and stocks, and opposite it, on the corner, a lovely house with gabled, two-storeyed porch. Pronounced 'Eden' and not 'eye-don', this is a delightfully unspoilt stone village.* Straight, not right, at road junction (SP - *Culworth*) *(but turn left if you wish to visit the small, much restored church, with views of handsome 18th-century Eydon Hall from its churchyard).*

(E) Near end of village, where road bends to left, go straight ahead through small gate and then through large metal gate. Through small gate still keeping in same direction, with fence on left and hedge on right. Soon starting to descend into broad valley of infant River Cherwell. At bottom of bridleway go over left-hand stile, temporarily leaving bridleway and continue in same direction into small spinney with hedge on right. Over footbridge crossing River Cherwell. *This flows into the Thames at Oxford and is the first south-flowing river we have encountered.* Bear left and continue up left-hand edge of field with river and later, hedge to immediate left and at end of field bear round to right and go through second gap in hedge to left.

52

(F) Through this gap, *where we are again joined by the Jurassic Way (see page 40) coming in from right (we shall share paths with this as far as Chipping Warden).* Now up track to immediate right of hedge and turn sharp left onto new track where our track bends to right at top of slope beyond line of Leylandii. Along track with trees to left and view of large pool down to left. Bear left onto surfaced farm road and where road bends to left heading for Wardenhill Farm, go straight ahead through gap onto track with hedge on right and large conifers on left. Soon pass derelict farm cottages on right and at end of field go through gate. Keep along top of field with fence to immediate left and slopes down to right. Bear slightly right away from fence line to aim for gate in hedge below.

(G) Through gate, cross minor road and through gate. Head along left-hand edge of field aiming for waymark just beyond small brook. Cross brook and head diagonally right aiming for stile on wood's edge. Cross stile and along wide track through wood. *Many derelict air-raid shelters here - there was a World War II airfield nearby.* Bear left at end of spinney and slightly left again onto surfaced road. Turn right onto road. Soon enter Chipping Warden passing Griffin Inn on right.

(H) Go straight ahead with care onto A361 by village green (SP - *Wardington*) *(but turn left if you wish to visit church or telephone box) (Now leaving Jurassic Way which goes to left here). Once a busy market town, 'Chipping' being the Old English word for market, Chipping Warden retains a flavour of times past. It has wide greens overlooked by thatched cottages and the remains of an old market cross near the impressive church.* Pass Rose and Crown Inn on right and turn right onto minor road (SP - *Appletree*). This road bends to left at end of village and then, where it bends slightly to right, go straight ahead, over stile and through area with caravans. Go to left of enclosure, over stile and along left-hand edge of field. Over stile into spinney and join track bearing diagonally left. Through gap and go diagonally slightly right along track. Continue in same direction across wide field to fence and stile behind large tree on right. Over stile and head diagonally left keeping to left of embanked pool near Churchlands (house), crossing possibly boggy ground. Through small gate at end of fence, turn right and shortly cross over two stiles plus possible electric fence. Continue straight ahead towards Highfield Farm keeping long hedge on immediate right. *Now entering Oxfordshire. Waymarks will be the standard 'Macmillan Green' from this point onwards.*

(J) Through metal gate, go across road by Highfield Farm and through gateway keeping to immediate right of low cowshed (now on permissive path). *If problem here refer to possible Update entry.* Go along field keeping as near as possible to left-hand hedge. Veer slightly right where hedge bends to right and soon go left through gateway. Now keep to right-hand edge of field and soon bear right through gap to go down outside, right-hand edge of wood. Through gateway at end of wood on left and turn sharp left, go about twenty yards and turn right (re-

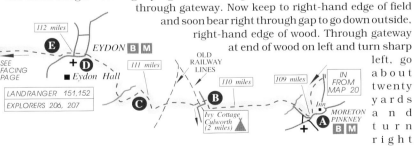

joining right-of-way) to head across field aiming just to right of oak tree in hedge ahead. Claydon now visible ahead, well beyond valley.

(A) Go across small bridge to right of oak tree and head diagonally left across long narrow field to probable waymark post in hedge to left. From waymark follow up field with small barn at end on right, keeping to immediate right of hedge. Through small gap in hedge in far left-hand corner of field and through next field keeping hedge on immediate left. At end of field bear slightly right and then left through large gap into next field keeping hedge on immediate left. Turn left at bottom of field, bear left over footbridge crossing stream and go diagonally across field aiming just to right of canal bridge.

The Oxford Canal, near Claydon

(B) Over stile and bear left onto road by small parking area to cross bridge over Oxford Canal. *(But go through gate by parking area and turn right onto Oxford Canal towpath if you wish to explore up to Claydon Top Lock.) The Oxford Canal, the work of James Brindley, was opened in 1790 to link the Coventry coal fields with the Thames at Oxford. Its towpath provides a fine walk over the watershed between the Midland Plain and the Thames Valley.* Now head westwards, straight up road and go straight, not left, at entry to Claydon (SP - *Claydon*). *Claydon is a quiet hilltop village less than two miles south of the point where the counties of Warwickshire, Northamptonshire and Oxfordshire meet. The little saddleback-towered church has Norman arcading with its supporting pillars no more than five feet high.* Bear round to right, pass Butlin Farm on right, with its very interesting Granary Museum of Bygones (don't miss this) and immediately go straight, not left by church (SP - *Boddington*).

(C) Pass telephone box on right and turn left onto small road opposite house called Latham. Go down quiet road and cross railway line with great care, noting warning signs stating 'STOP, LOOK, LISTEN Beware of trains'. Now entering Warwickshire. Go along farm track and pass large poultry farm on right.

(D) Now cross busy A423 with great care. Over stile in hedge next to signpost, almost opposite but slightly to left, and head diagonally left across field. Over footbridge and through gap in hedge and bear slightly left aiming to left of houses near entry to Farnborough. Bear left at end of houses and follow round edge of playing-field, turning right at its far end before turning left onto road.

MAP 22

Scale

0   1/2   1   One Mile

To Avon Dassett
1 mile   **B** **M**

FROM FACING PAGE

E

120 miles

TO WARWICK

SEE MAP 23

F

B4100

Village Green

B4086

WARMINGTON
B **M**

M40

© Crown copyright

TO BANBURY

Follow road through village passing Butchers Arms and telephone box on left and pathway up to church on left. *Farnborough is a charming Hornton-stone, hillside village with cottages and houses poised above its winding street. Although its spire is Victorian, the rest of the church is medieval and worth visiting. The National Trust's Farnborough Hall is a handsome, largely 18th-century house in modest parkland, the outstanding feature of which is its lovely terraced walk, complete with*

Farnborough Hall

temple, pavilion and obelisk. Try to visit this if open. Bear right at road junction near entrance to Farnborough Hall (SP - *Avon Dassett*) and soon bear left at next road junction down Dassett Road. *Good views of Farnborough Hall up to left and of lake to right, with wide grass verges either side. View of further lake down through trees to left and eventually there are views back to buildings and obelisk on Farnborough Terrace on hill slope to left.*

(E) Turn left onto smaller, unfenced road and go some distance before crossing bridge over M40 motorway. Turn right off road immediately beyond top of motorway bridge, down steps and over stile. Head diagonally across field to its far left-hand side. Turn left in far corner of field, over footbridge and immediately turn right to cross 2nd footbridge. Now head diagonally left keeping well to left of sewage works. Over stile, cross roadway, over footbridge and continue in same direction across narrow field. Over stile and over yet another stile before turning right onto road at entry to Warmington. *We now enter the Cotswolds 'Area of Outstanding Natural Beauty' and, apart from a brief exit to Shenington, we shall travel through it until reaching a point beyond Box in Wiltshire (see page 91, Point G).*

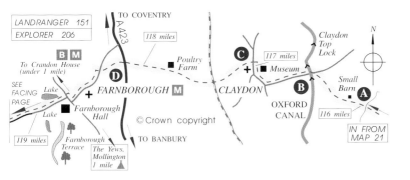

(F) Bear left and up road across village green. *This wide sloping green is complete with pond and sheep dip and is overlooked by a series of delightful Hornton stone houses and cottages, including an early-17th-century manor house and an elegant little Georgian rectory.* Pass Plough Inn on right and just beyond, leave road as it bears to right and go straight ahead up footpath steps, with churchyard on right. *The church stands in a churchyard shaded by pine trees and within will be found some very attractive rood loft stairs, Norman north and south arcading and a number of other interesting features.* Turn right onto footpath and go beside still busy B4100 at top of hill with church on right.

(A) Leave Warmington church and go down hill on footpath beside still busy B4100. Soon cross entry to minor road coming in from right and just beyond first house on left of B4100, cross with great care and go up sloping driveway. Immediately turn right to go over stile and turn left to follow fence-line on immediate left. Pass house on left, through metal gate, between bushes and over stile built through second metal gate. Go between fences with farm buildings over to left. Through gate by water trough and keep in same direction along upper terrace with fence on immediate left. Splendid views out over the Avon valley including Farnborough Hall and the Burton Dassett Hills but sadly, with much noise from the M40. Pass solitary beech tree poised above scarp face to right. At end of fence, over stile and turn left to head for metal gate below transformer on power-poles.

(B) Through gate, over B4086 and head slightly left to go through gate onto track with hedge on right. After about 100 yards turn right, through double metal gates and down steep slope to stile in fence at bottom. Keep in same direction heading for gap below oak tree on right. Keep in same direction across large field.

(C) Over stile beside large gateway crossing line of stream and bear left onto track between parallel hedge-lines. Bear round to right, keeping on track and turn left through gateway, go steeply up field following line of power-poles, aiming just to left of power-pole on skyline. Over stile beside horse-jump at top of hill and bear right, down terraced field to remains of stile to left of gateway in valley bottom, keeping to right of line of power-poles. Over stile and head up hill aiming to left of farm buildings and over stile by power-pole.

(D) Leave field and go left down surfaced farm drive into Ratley. Pass Rose and Crown Inn on left and bear slightly left by small triangular green. *A small, well sheltered village, Ratley has a grey stone church almost entirely in the Decorated style and a medieval cross in its churchyard.* Pass church on left, bear round to right keeping on road through village. *Earthwork up to left (on private ground) is known as 'The Mount' and was probably a gun emplacement built just before the nearby Battle of Edgehill (1642).* Leave Ratley going straight up road (SP - *Edgehill*).

(E) At T-junction cross road, into woodland joining the Centenary Way, which we shall follow for approximately two-and-a-half-miles. *Developed by Warwickshire County Council, this 98-mile recreational path runs from Kingsbury, south of Tamworth to Meon Hill, north of Chipping Campden.* Down steep steps known as Jacob's Ladder and bear left keeping in woodlands, **not** going through gate into field. *Good views of Radway Grange in its parkland down to right. This was once the home of Sanderson Miller, 18th-century gentleman architect and one of the pioneers of the neo-Gothick style.* Fork left up track when drawing level with obelisk

The Vale of Red Horse from beyond Sunrising Hill

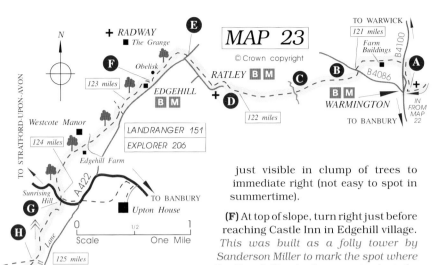

SEE
MAP 24

just visible in clump of trees to immediate right (not easy to spot in summertime).

(F) At top of slope, turn right just before reaching Castle Inn in Edgehill village. *This was built as a folly tower by Sanderson Miller to mark the spot where the Royal Standard was raised at the outset of the Battle of Edgehill, on Sunday, October 23rd, 1642. There are fine views from the inn's terrace garden over the site of the battlefield and the Vale of Red Horse. Phone box just to north of inn.* Go down steep path behind Castle Inn, with railings to right. At bottom, bear left into woodlands and follow path along woods until joining track coming up from right. *This is known as King John's Lane, an old road that once came up from Kineton - where there is a mound known as King John's Castle. Sadly, there is no proven connection with that most maligned of all monarchs.* Immediately after junction with King John's Lane bear right, off it, onto narrow path between fence and upper edge of woods. Keep on clearly defined path for half-a-mile. Bear left up tarmac drive and after a few yards bear right keeping to immediate right of Edgehill Farm's building and not down concrete roadway. Continue to follow path along upper edge of woods for another half-a-mile.

(G) Just beyond laurel bushes, go briefly but definitely left and cross busy A422 with great care. *Top of Sunrising Hill just to right. Layby car park with phone box 100 yards up to left. To visit National Trust's Upton House, walk up A422 beyond layby and immediately after this road bends to left, go across it to follow footpath over fields - half-a-mile. This handsome William and Mary mansion contains an outstanding collection of works of art and also has very pleasant, steep, sloping gardens.* Back on main route, after crossing A422 go down farm drive almost opposite, turn right down drive well before farm buildings, then left by post-and-rail fence and immediately fork left keeping on upper path. Through young plantation and metal gate into terrace-like open field with steep slopes to right and superb views over the Vale of Red Horse towards Bredon Hill and the distant Malverns. *The Vale of Red Horse takes its name from a hill figure which was once cut into hill slopes somewhere just south of here.* Keep across this field with fence to immediate left, and at its end, go through gate onto narrow path between hedge on left and wood on right.

(H) At junction of paths go straight ahead with fence on left and wood on right *(do **not** fork right down hill; the Centenary Way does, but we leave it here).* Now on special permissive path - not a right-of-way. Keep along path, eventually dropping down to farm drive in wood and turning left up drive, thereby re-joining right-of-way. Go up and along drive to arrive at road (Sugarswell Lane).

(A) Go straight across Sugarswell Lane, a sometimes busy minor road, and onto farm track. Keep down track between fences, almost immediately re-entering Oxfordshire. At end of track go through metal gate into field and keep along its crooked right-hand edge. *Pleasant views of valley down to right - this drains southwards as we have again crossed the watershed between the Severn and the Thames tributaries.* Over stile beside metal gate and keep down right-hand edge of field. Through hunting gate and keep straight in same direction down across field in now wide valley aiming for right-hand edge of wood coming down from left.

(B) Over concrete platform spanning dry hollow and veer half-right aiming to right of single oak tree and through wooden gate. Now keep to right-hand edge of field with stream immediately below to right. At end of field go through gap to immediate left of small building, but if ground impossibly boggy, use gate a few yards up to left. Then bear right to go through large wooden gate (or just a gap!) just below right hand edge of coniferous wood. Along short track to right of wood, through second gate and keep in same direction across field. Shenington church tower soon visible over to right. Through metal gate, head for horse-jumps in middle of field and keep in same direction beyond them, aiming for gate in hedge ahead.

(C) Go through gate. *We are joined here by the d'Arcy Dalton Way, which comes in from left. This 65-mile recreational route runs southwards from the Oxford Canal near Wormleighton to link with the Ridgeway Long Distance Path near Wayland's Smithy. We shall follow it for about three miles, until reaching Epwell.* Keep straight, parallel with upper, wooded edge of field, along slight terrace, which becomes more track-like at its latter end as it heads slightly downwards. Through metal gate and head down across field, around right-hand side of riding school area and veering slightly right to head for stile to right of low stone wall. Alkerton Church (see below) visible up to left. Over stile and through small boggy spinney (known locally as `the osier beds') to go over two stiles with sleeper bridge between, crossing the Sor Brook. Go up field keeping to right of group of poplar trees and to immediate left of small, fenced orchard.

(D) Over stile at entry to Shenington and soon turn right onto road. *Standing over 500 feet above sea level, Shenington is a large, stone and thatch village grouped around a wide green. Its church was heavily restored in the 19th century by J.L.Pearson, best known as architect of Truro Cathedral. Neighbouring Alkerton, across the valley, has a smaller church but this has a real flavour of medieval times. If time allows, why not visit this and also the attractive garden of nearby Brook Cottage.* Pass Shenington church and school on left and keep on widest road across village green, with Bell Inn over to right. Keep straight out of village on road and immediately after last bungalow on left, bear left off road and over stile.

Valley beyond Sugarswell Lane

(E) Go down field keeping to immediate right of fence. Over bridge crossing stream and head up bank to top left-hand corner of field. Streams here flow south and east to the Cherwell, thence to the Thames. Over stile by gate at top of field. Keep to immediate right of fence line and through small gate at end of field. Drop down into valley, following slight signs of stony track, to cross bridge over stream. Note ancient terracing especially to left. Through gateway and head diagonally left along slight signs of track with pool well down to left. Over stile crossing fence and go slightly left heading for near left-hand end of next fence line to cross a small bridge. Go diagonally for about 25 paces to small stile in hedge and go diagonally up across field and once over brow, drop into valley aiming for waymark in far right-hand corner of field. Over bridge across minute brook and head up hill diagonally right, aiming for highest power-pole. Go to far left corner of field aiming to left of farm buildings and over stile onto road.

(F) Turn left onto road by Yarn Hill Farm and almost immediately turn right through metal gate (SP - *Epwell*) and onto farm track first keeping to less muddy, left-hand side and then following hedge-line on right. This track is heading between Yarn Hill on left and Epwell Hill on right. About 120 yards short of the next gate watch out for possible loose fitting drain cover in grass - it could be very dangerous. Through large metal gate and continue to left of hedge-line. Epwell village now visible ahead. Over three stiles crossing wooden fences and following hedge-line to right (ignore waymarked stile in hedge to right) and after third stile head diagonally left across small field with brook on right, then cross brook to post on edge of garden. Cross this quietly and through gate into Epwell.

(G) Bear left on road by village green, over footbridge beside ford and up road to centre of Epwell. *This small Hornton-stone village with its modest little church and welcoming inn is tucked away in a hollow amongst small bumpy hills.* Pass telephone box on left and bear right by village hall on right. Bear left on road (sign - *Max Width 7'0'*) keeping churchyard on left (footpath to Chandler's Arms on left beyond churchyard) *(We leave the d'Arcy Dalton Way here).* Soon after our road bends to right, turn left onto footpath between private gardens. Bear slightly right in field and head up to left of hedge-line. Over stile at end of field *(crossing the ill-defined course of a Roman road that ran from Alcester and Stratford towards Kings Sutton, south of Banbury)* and turn right and then left to follow right-hand edge of field aiming for radio mast on horizon. (Ignore way-marks on stile to right.) Through metal gate and keep in same direction.

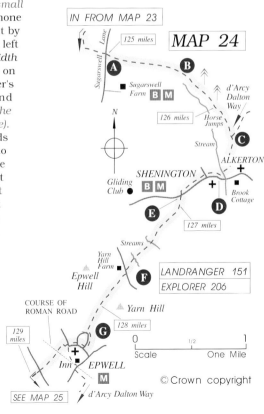

IN FROM MAP 23

Sugarswell Lane

125 miles

MAP 24

A B

Sugarswell Farm B M

d'Arcy Dalton Way

N

126 miles

Horse Jumps

Stream

C

ALKERTON

SHENINGTON

Gliding Club ●

B M

D

Brook Cottage

E

127 miles

Streams

Yarn Hill Farm

Epwell Hill

F

LANDRANGER 151

EXPLORER 206

COURSE OF ROMAN ROAD

Yarn Hill

129 miles

G

128 miles

0 1/2 1

Scale One Mile

© Crown copyright

Inn EPWELL

M

SEE MAP 25

d'Arcy Dalton Way

59

(A) Through large wooden gate, turn right onto road and very soon turn left through metal gate. Head straight across field aiming to right of radio mast and over stile about 50 yards to right of mast. Turn left onto Ditchedge Lane, *a green road that here forms the boundary between Oxfordshire and Warwickshire. This trackway may have been part of a prehistoric trade route, but it is more likely to have Anglo-Saxon origins. Although there is now no ditch alongside it, there may once have been one marking the boundary between the two counties.* We shall now follow Ditchedge Lane for some two-and-a-half miles and route-finding will be comparatively simple. Much of the lane is on a ridge and there are fine views both to right and left. Pass radio mast on left and into more sheltered length of lane, with pleasant glimpses to right of the spire of Winderton church, the impressive tower of Brailes church and Brailes Hill, topped with its clump of trees.

(B) Go straight ahead joining B4035 for short distance, before bearing left at next bend just beyond Warwickshire County sign, re-joining Ditchedge Lane. Keep straight along this green road with its fine views both to left and right. At end of third field on left, pass unsigned bridleway to left running between parallel hedges and leading to Sibford Gower - a possible diversion. *It would be possible to re-join main route further along Ditchedge Lane, or beyond Traitor's Ford.* Just beyond Round Hill to right, at end of hedge-bordered section of Ditchedge Lane, through gate into field following same line as lane and still following county boundary, with hedge to immediate left. Now start to drop down into upper valley of River Stour with fine views over to right including Broadway Tower, on the distant Cotswold skyline almost due west. At bottom of long field follow path along small sunken section of track and through gate onto minor road.

(C) Bear left and over bridge beside attractive ford with woodland on both sides of road. *This is known as Traitor's Ford, but the origins of its name are shrouded in mystery - some think that a traitor was killed here, others believe that it was once known as Traders' Ford, the traders using it during their journeys with pack animals along Ditchedge Lane.* Up wooded hill on minor road, soon going straight, not left, at first road junction (SP - *Whichford*) and then turning right at second road junction (SP - *Whichford*). Keep on minor road for about half-a-mile.

(D) At first hedge-line on left beyond New Barn farm buildings turn left through gateway. Go up track keeping to immediate left of fence and hedge-line. Bear right over stile and go through second gate (first gate nearly always locked).. Go half right, follow slight signs of track down field and over stile beside gate at bottom of field. Down hill keeping to left of scanty hedge and tree line and at its end, bear half-left heading for bottom left-hand corner of field. Over stile and bridge, up small lane into quiet valley hamlet of Ascott and soon turn right onto path immediately beyond gates of first house on right. Up narrow path between hedge and fence and over

small stile into old orchard. Over second stile and turn left onto minor cul-de-sac road.

(E) Turn right at x-rds by Coombe House and follow path beside minor road heading towards Whichford. Bear left at road junction by small triangular green (Sign - *Ascott Corner*) and enter Whichford, *an unspoilt village below the steep scarp face of the Oxfordshire Cotswolds.* Keep straight, not left, at wide village green

Traitor's Ford

(SP - *Stourton*) and pass Norman Knight Inn on right. Bear left by War Memorial at end of green with telephone box on left. Pass elegant 18th-century Old Rectory on right and church just beyond on right. *Whichford church has a Norman south doorway, an early 14th-century tower and a beautiful Perpendicular clerestory.*

(F) Well beyond church turn left up Roman Row - a small housing estate. Remains of medieval moat visible over to right at this junction. Over stile on left at end of Roman Row. Continue in same direction with hedge on right and at end of hedge turn half-right to go diagonally up hill following imprecise track towards oak and ash tree. Beyond these trees, keep just outside left-hand edge of Whichford Wood for about a mile, passing through gaps in two cross hedges before reaching an X-roads of tracks. (Now keep alert - some walkers have gone wrong here!) (Waymarks have sometimes been removed.) Keep straight ahead on track now going between a tall hedge to its left and wood still to its right. But after about 200 yards veer right as track fully enters wood and drops down into valley.

(G) After nearly a quarter-of-a-mile turn left just beyond valley bottom onto track leading down valley. Through gateway at end of woods into field, keeping on track along right-hand edge of field with hedge and fence to immediate right. Long Compton church visible in valley ahead. Through metal gate beyond woods on right, still keeping on track, with hedge now to immediate left and open field up to right. Through gate at end of field and continue on harder surfaced track, which is now between two high hedges. Through metal gate and head straight across field passing large pond on left (Signed - 'Danger') and through metal gate to left of house. Onto surfaced driveway at entry to Long Compton and turn left with care onto A3400 (SP - *Woodstock*).

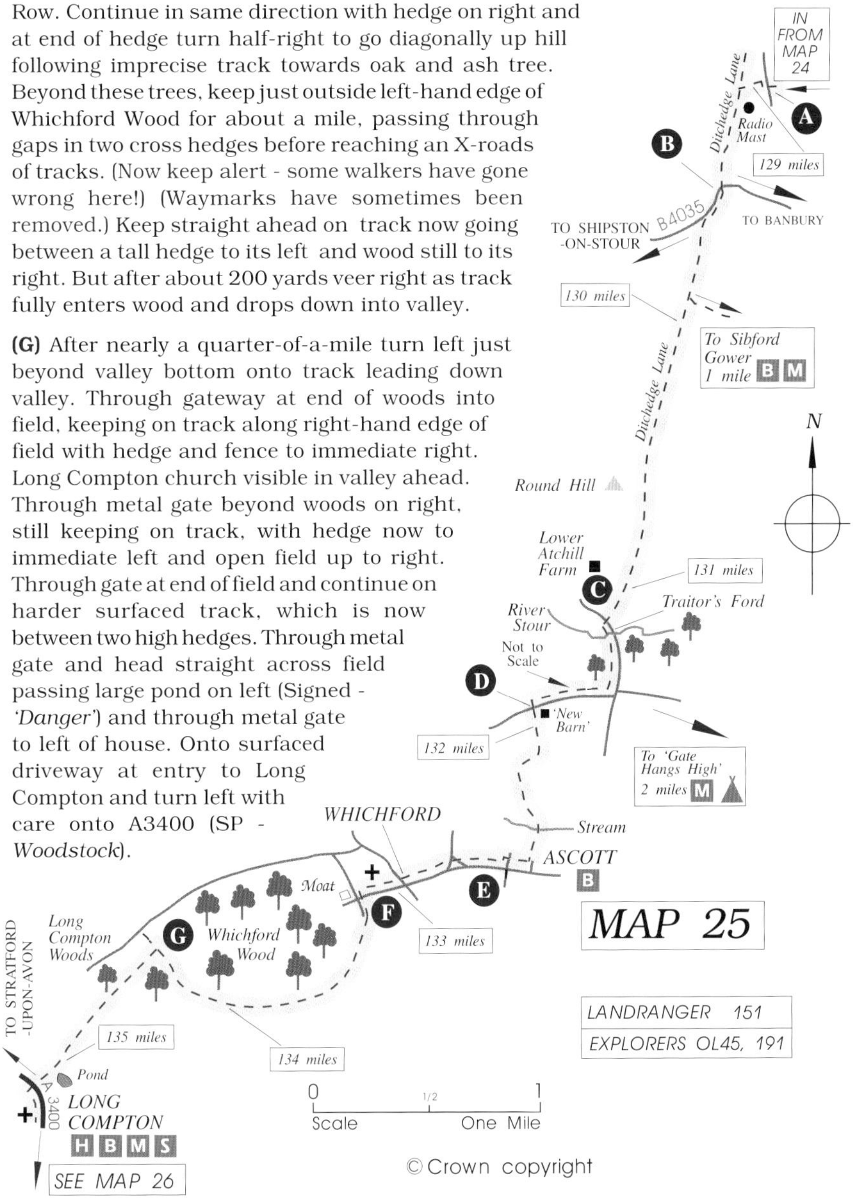

IN FROM MAP 24

Ditchedge Lane

Radio Mast

A

B

129 miles

TO SHIPSTON -ON-STOUR

B4035

TO BANBURY

130 miles

To Sibford Gower 1 mile **B** **M**

Ditchedge Lane

N

Round Hill

Lower Atchill Farm

C

131 miles

Traitor's Ford

River Stour

Not to Scale

D

■ 'New Barn'

132 miles

To 'Gate Hangs High' 2 miles **M**

WHICHFORD

Stream

ASCOTT **B**

E

MAP 25

Moat

+

F

133 miles

TO STRATFORD -UPON-AVON

Long Compton Woods

G

Whichford Wood

| LANDRANGER | 151 |
| EXPLORERS | OL45, 191 |

135 miles

134 miles

0   1/2   1
Scale   One Mile

Pond

A3400

+

LONG COMPTON

H **B** **M** **S**

SEE MAP 26

© Crown copyright

(A) Having turned left onto A3400, follow it through Long Compton, keeping to pathway on left. *Sitting beneath the high Cotswold edge, Long Compton has many attractive stone houses and cottages strung out along the still busy A3400.* Pass Crockwell Street on right *(go down here and soon onto path if you wish to use camp site at Mill Farm - three-quarters-of-a-mile).* **Pass church on right with its handsome Perpendicular tower and charming thatched lych-gate.** Manor House (B&B) on left, Post Office Stores on right. Base of old cross on stone plinth on right just beyond. *Stop to look at interesting Millennium Cross and Sundial on left.* Pass road to left signed B&B, which leads to telephone box and to Butler's Road Farm.

(B) Just beyond this road junction, turn right off A3400 beyond Village Hall on right, going through wooden gate with stone gate pier to left inscribed 'Daddy's Bank'. *(But go straight ahead for few yards if you wish to visit Red Lion Hotel and Restaurant.)* Through second wooden gate and head slightly left across field, first going on part of concrete track, to go through gate in wooden fence. Keep in same direction to go over stile beside metal gate, then go left and turn immediately right to follow well surfaced private road with hedge to right *(it may be possible to follow path to right of hedge - if so, this will be clearly marked)*. Leave surfaced track where it bends to right and continue in same direction on rougher track keeping hedge and ditch on immediate right and passing large converted barn beyond hedge on right. Where track bends to right, go straight ahead up field and then bear slightly left to head for far left-hand, top corner.

(C) Over stile at this corner and head diagonally up hill across field following well used path, keeping to immediate right of spring. South Hill Farm soon visible ahead. Through metal gate and first head towards centre of farm buildings, but soon converging with hedge line on right. Bear right over stile and follow line of hedge on right, with farm buildings to left. Where hedge finishes, keep in same direction across field, aiming well to right of radio mast with reflectors.

(D) Over stone stile and join road keeping in same direction and return briefly into Oxfordshire. *(But if you wish to visit the Bronze Age stone circle known as the Rollright Stones, turn left onto road, go straight, not left, turn left and go straight not left again - about one mile. This diversion is worthwhile and not as difficult to reach as the route directions would imply!)* Back on main route again - fine views westwards to Gloucestershire Cotswolds over to right. Just beyond point where road bends to right, go through metal gate on left (back into Warwickshire) and immediately bear right onto bridleway to follow along left-hand side of wall, thus continuing in same general direction. Oakham Farm soon visible down to right and good views ahead right, out over Evenlode Valley. Soon, near point where wall comes in from right, cross to right-hand side of our parallel wall, but continue in same direction. Follow farm track in same direction for about a mile with Little Compton visible down to right. *(Watch for left turn onto bridleway if you wish to visit Cross Hands Inn - meals, camping.)* Through small metal gate beside large one below power-

Chastleton House

pole with transformer, and note sign beyond on left regarding quarry workings. Keep in same direction with quarry to left and wall to right.

(E) Pass quarry and farm buildings on left, cross busy A44 with great care and onto minor road. Entrance to Grey Goose Farm on left of main route just beyond A44. Through gate beside cattle-grid onto unfenced road, having just re-entered Oxfordshire and through pleasant parkland with grass and trees (Notice states - *Private Property - No Parking, Camping or Picnicking Please*). Pass two farmhouses down to right and at end of unfenced road through gate ignoring bridleway sign to left, and turn right onto minor road.

(F) Go down hill and keep on road passing NT car park* on left and Chastleton Church and House on right. (*But if car park is open and in use, turn left into it. Go past small hut and by kind permission of the National Trust go down path across pleasant field and close to attractive 18th-century arched dovecote *(This is not a right-of-way. Please leave all gates as you find them).* Turn left onto road and pass Chastleton House on right re-joining route. *Extensively restored by the National Trust, this fine Stuart manor house was probably designed by Robert Smythson, the architect best known for Hardwick Hall in Derbyshire. It has a handsome five-gabled south front and an interior largely undisturbed by 18th- or 19th-century alteration, the most impressive feature of which is its Long Gallery at the top of the house.* After about 100 paces turn left through large wooden gate *(not signed, as use of this next short section is kindly allowed for Macmillan Way walkers only, by the National Trust and the owner of nearby Harcombe, and is not a right-of-way).* Through second wooden gate, up lovely avenue of trees and soon go through small metal gate passing from Oxfordshire into Gloucestershire and returning to right-of-way.

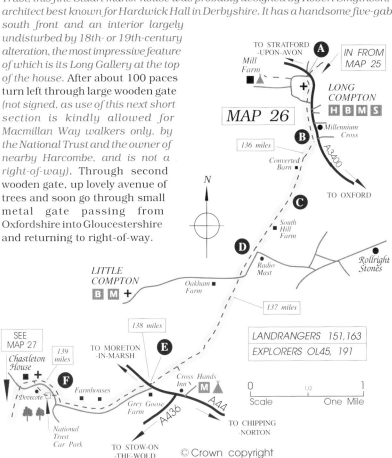

MAP 26

136 miles

137 miles

138 miles

139 miles

LANDRANGERS 151,163
EXPLORERS OL45, 191

0   1/2   1
Scale   One Mile

© Crown copyright

(A) Now head diagonally right, across field on well used track. Stow-on-the-Wold church just visible on skyline over to right. Over brow and start to drop down heading for waymark to left of two trees. Over stile by wooden gate beyond waymark and continue in same direction down field. Over stile following right-hand of two waymarks and continue down field keeping fairly close to right of hedge-line. Beyond large tree near end of field, bear left over stile, and immediately bear right, now keeping to left of remaining hedge-line and keeping in same direction. Soon over another stile with hedge converging from left. Initially follow line of hedge to immediate right, but where it bends to right, head diagonally left across field aiming for waymark on stile. Over this stile and onto track with hedge to left.

(B) Pass farm buildings on right and at entry to Adlestrop go over road junction onto minor road by bus shelter with the old Adlestrop Railway Station sign board on left. *This stands as a tribute to Edward Thomas, whose highly evocative poem Adlestrop, begins thus, 'Yes, I remember Adlestrop ...'. Sadly he died in France in 1917, aged only 39. His poem is recorded on a plaque on the seat.* Follow minor road into pretty Adlestrop village with its flower-filled cottage gardens and bear right (SP - Church). Bear right by church and then bear left down track between churchyard wall and Old Rectory; *this was often visited by Jane Austen, when her uncle, Theophilus Leigh, lived here.* Through small gate keeping on track between fences, with small lakes possibly just visible ahead and over to right. *Views back to Adlestrop Park, the south-west front of which was designed by Sanderson Miller of Radway (see page 57).* Through small gate beside large one and head diagonally right on track to immediate left of cricket pitch's low boundary fence. Skirt round about a third of cricket pitch's perimeter and turn right, off track just beyond large trees aiming well to left of trees bordering probably invisible lake. Head for footpath fingerpost now visible ahead.

(C) Over two stiles and turn left onto minor road. Almost immediately turn right with care onto A436 and keep on path along its right-hand side. *Over bridge crossing Isambard K. Brunel's London to Worcester railway line, with view to right of remains of station immortalised by Edward Thomas (see above).* Then over infant River Evenlode and soon cross to path on left-hand side of road. Turn left onto minor road (SP - *Lower Oddington*) and soon enter attractive village of Lower Oddington. Follow round long bend to right by Fox Inn and turn left at road junction (Small SP on wall - *St Nicholas Church*).

(D) At bottom of hill, turn right just before drive to New Rectory Farm on right, and over stile by gateway where road bends to left in valley. *But go straight ahead for 250 yards if you wish to visit fascinating St Nicholas's Church. This is an ambitious, largely 13th- and 14th-century building with a remarkably unspoilt interior. See especially the lovely old chancel roof and the extensive 'Doom' wall paintings.* Back on main route - go straight across middle of narrow field, through kissing-gate and continue in same direction keeping to immediate right of hedge. Through another kissing-gate, cross small brook and up narrow pathway between two walls with house

Memories of Edward Thomas at Adlestrop

on right. Join road at eastern end of Upper Oddington and continue in same direction passing drive on left to Latimer Farm. Bear left at road junction just beyond and up road for about a quarter-of-a-mile, with Horse and Groom Inn on right and telephone box on left.

(E) Keep on road out of Upper Oddington and turn right over stile just beyond last house on right. Down grass walk between two fences, over stile and head diagonally left aiming for yellow waymark just below power-pole in hedge across field. Do not go over waymarked stile but turn left through a metal gate to follow up to left of hedge. Where hedge turns to right, continue up across field aiming just to left of grass-covered reservoir. *Good views back from here include distant Brailes Hill, with its clump of trees and, much closer, Warren Hastings' beloved Daylesford House, built by him after retiring from his controversial career as Governor of Bengal.* Turn right through kissing gate to left of reservoir and go between reservoir fence on right and hedge on left. Into field keeping to immediate right of hedge and follow this line behind rugby club's pavilion and along left-hand edge of club's grounds for about 30 paces. Soon turn left up bank, through wooden gate and go along grassy track.

(F) Turn right onto B4450 and walk carefully along here on right-hand side to face oncoming traffic - road is quite busy and verges are narrow. Soon pass Fairview Farmhouse on right and good view of Stow-on-the-Wold church ahead. Turn left off B4450 just before reaching the A436 (SP - *Maugersbury Village only*). Follow road into Maugersbury, *a pleasant village with lovely views across valley to Icomb Hill.*

(G) Bear left in Maugersbury by small green and telephone box on right (SP - *Maugersbury only*). *(But turn right if you wish to visit Stow-on-the-Wold - half-a-mile. To re-join main route at Map 28, Point A, walk down path beside A429 Fosse Way.) The attractive little market town of Stow-on-the-Wold is the focal point of the northern Cotswolds. Its Market Square is lively with visitors and local country shoppers and it has all the facilities required by users of our Way including an excellent Tourist Information Centre and a number of B&Bs, hotels, inns and eating places.* Main route bears round to right in Maugersbury keeping Dower House on left. Pass Manor Farm on right and walk out of village on road despite twin *No Through Road* signs.

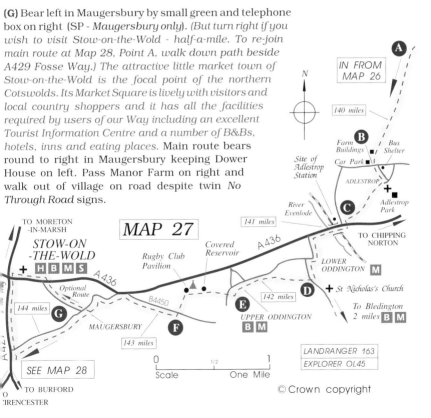

65

(A) About a mile beyond Maugersbury, through road barrier and turn left to follow wide path down beside the very busy A429 (SP - *Cirencester*). (If you have taken the diversion via Stow-on-the-Wold, re-join the main route here.) *The A429 follows the course of the Fosse Way. This was built by the Romans a few years after their invasion of Britain in AD43 and ran for 182 miles, between Lincoln and Exeter. For much of its course the Macmillan Way runs parallel with the Fosse Way and it crosses it twice - here below Stow, and later, near Castle Combe in Wiltshire.* At bottom of hill turn right and cross A429 by traffic lights with great care. Go down left-hand of two drives (SP's - *Private Drive to Hyde Mill* and *Bridleway to Lower Swell*). Follow well surfaced road past woodlands, cottage and farm to arrive at gate into Hyde Mill driveway. Go through gate and between avenue of poplars before bearing right by Hyde Mill House.

(B) Turn left over bridge (SP - *Lower Swell, Lower Slaughter*) crossing mill pound *(this is formed by the Dikler, a stream which rises at Donnington Brewery lake and which, at Bourton-on-the-Water, flows into the River Eye, itself a tributary of the better known Windrush. We shall now start to encounter the waymarks of The Heart of England Way, the Donnington Way, the Monarch's Way and the Gloucestershire Way, all of which converge on Lower Slaughter.* Keep straight past houses, then bear left (SP - *Lower Slaughter*). Bear right at end of last house (SP - *Lower Slaughter*) and along track. Over very small stream, turn left through kissing gate and go straight across field (very boggy here in winter), with little River Dikler on left. Over stile with Dikler just to left and head across field towards next gate with the Dikler veering away to left. Through gate and continue in same direction to cross fenced ditch before changing direction slightly to right. Cross another fenced ditch and almost immediately through gateway.

(C) Now head diagonally aiming for waymark by gateway near end of left-hand edge of field. Through gateway (SP - *Lower Slaughter*) and head for stile and gate at bottom right-hand corner of field. Through stile to right of gate and head diagonally across short field aiming for waymark. Over small bridge and stile and turn right to follow round edge of field before shortly turning left in corner, with wood now to right. Now aim straight towards Lower Slaughter Manor (now a hotel) along a broad grassy headland with hedge to immediate right. But just before end of field, turn right through metal gate and then immediately left, with hedge now on left, thus maintaining previous line. Over stile and into cricket field keeping to its left-hand edge.

(D) Through small wooden gate behind cricket pavilion onto path at entry to Lower Slaughter. Now bear right onto driveway and then bear left onto road by corner of churchyard. Pass church on left and bear right at road junction by Washbourne Court Hotel (SP - *Upper Slaughter*). *Now briefly*

Lower Slaughter

on the Wardens' Way - a 14-mile walking route between Bourton-on-the-Water and Winchcombe. Walk up village on quieter, right-hand side of stream - the little River Eye, which flows into the River Windrush just below Bourton-on-the-Water. *Most of this delightful and much visited village seems almost to have been planted upon the banks of its stream. Stop here awhile if you are fortunate enough to arrive here at a quiet time.* Cross stream by small stone bridge (but go straight ahead if you wish to visit the interesting Old Mill Museum and Shop). Over 'main road' onto smaller road by Kingswell Cottage *(Now leaving the Wardens' Way).* Leave Lower Slaughter and climb out of valley, but do look back at mill with its water wheel and little brick chimney.

(E) At T-junction cross minor road with care and onto track. Pass small wood in field to left as track levels out. Views of bustling Bourton-on-the-Water well over to left. Start gentle descent into Windrush Valley and cross road to go through small gate. *The road we have just crossed is known as Buckle Street. It acquired its name in Anglo-Saxon times, but its origins are probably much earlier.* Head diagonally right across large field aiming for far right-hand corner and go through small metal gate.

(F) Bear left onto well defined track with wall to left and soon through large metal gate. Keep on track with wall to immediate left (still dropping down into valley) and then through metal gate and down track, now overhung with trees, with narrow field to right. Bear right at junction of bridleways, *joining the Windrush Way - a 14-mile walking route between Winchcombe and Bourton-on-the-Water.* Down wide, surfaced path curving left to surfaced road with houses on right. Over River Windrush and immediately start to climb out of valley. Bear slightly left by entrance roadway to Aston Farm on right, *now leaving the Windrush Way. Almost no sign is now visible of railway line that once crossed road here.* Almost immediately bear right keeping on surfaced road, ignoring waymark on left. Up steep little pitch and then turn right, off road, to walk up field to immediate right of hedge and wall, which soon bears left by tree. Pleasant views back over the Windrush Valley from here.

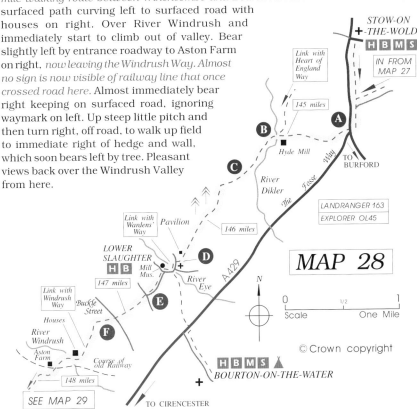

(A) Cross the busy A436 with great care, through double metal gates and keep to left-hand edge of field with wall on immediate left. *Now traversing some classic 'Cotswold country', with rolling wolds and wide open views; and if it's early summer, skylarks will almost certainly be singing above.* Pass attractive clump of trees over to left which are sited on top of a Stone Age long barrow or burial mound. Follow hedge-line as it curves down to right and then bear left through gap in wall, to farm track with buildings of Camp Farm down to right. Turn left onto track and almost immediately turn right to go across sleeper bridge by gap in hedge. Go diagonally left across corner of field and then follow up left-hand side of field with hedge to left. Through gap in cross-hedge converging from right, still keeping to left-hand edge of field.

(B) Bear right onto minor road just beyond small wood on left. (We shall now follow road into Cold Aston, with its church soon visible over to right.) Down hill into valley with woods soon on both sides and up road, noting alternative name for this village on its entry sign - Aston Blank. *Having visited this high wold village in winter, we feel that its usual name 'Cold Aston' is totally justifiable!* Bear half-left at Cold Aston's village green with its massive sycamore tree, telephone box and delightful inn, the Plough; taking small road to immediate left of inn. *But go straight ahead if you wish to visit the interesting, largely Norman church, with pleasant stone vaulting beneath its tower.* Keep straight past cottage on right called *Alberts* and over low stone stile at end of small road. Down narrow path with fence to left and wall to right, over second stile and turn right keeping fence on immediate right. Over third (stone) stile and through gate to pass in front of house with small ha-ha bordered lawn on right.

(C) Over fourth (stone) stile and bear left onto Bangup Lane, a surfaced track happily signed *Unfit for Motor Vehicles*, which we shall follow as far as Turkdean. Soon pass Bangup Cottage and Bangup Barn on right. After one-and-a-half miles go up attractive sunken road overhung with trees at entry to Turkdean.

(D) Turn left onto road by small triangular green in Turkdean and go through village. Pass telephone box. *On left pass church in large churchyard bordered by horse-chestnut trees. The interior has several interesting features including a Norman chancel arch and a medieval stone pulpit.* Turn right where road bends to left beyond sunken horse-trough on right, onto sunken footpath overhung with trees which

leads down hill (take care here - slippery and steep). Soon enter hamlet of Lower Dean on track with house on left. Over small bridge crossing stream, pass post box on right and bear right onto road by house over to left. Up hill on road leaving Lower Dean, soon passing Castle Barn Farm on left and woods on right.

Bangup Lane, well beyond Cold Aston

(E) Straight, not right at minor road junction (SP - *Hampnett*) and immediately cross busy A40 with care, to join minor road (SP - *Hampnett village only*). Pass Hampnett entry sign and start to drop down into this minute village, its wide green having houses thinly spread around it. Through gate to go on road through village, soon passing trough on left of road which is source of River Leach. *This flows south-eastwards from here to join the Thames near Lechlade. The nearby, largely Norman church has an unusual interior decorated in 'medieval style' in the 1880s.* Just before reaching church (ahead left) turn right by telephone box onto small road leading down hill (SP - *No Through Road*). *(But go straight ahead, past church and then bear half-right onto path down valley if you wish to visit Northleach, with its Countryside Museum, Mechanical Music Museum and fine wool church - one mile).*

(F) Back on main route (having turned right by telephone box) go down hill keeping on surfaced road where infant River Leach flows beneath it. Now go to left and almost immediately turn right onto path just before road becomes private drive. Up path with walls on both sides and through wooden gate into field. Route is now straight ahead to corner of wall ahead, then along fence/hedge on right-hand edge of field and then down slope to go through small gate. Straight across field in deep valley aiming for stile just to left of junction of wall lines. Over stile and keep to immediate left of wall.

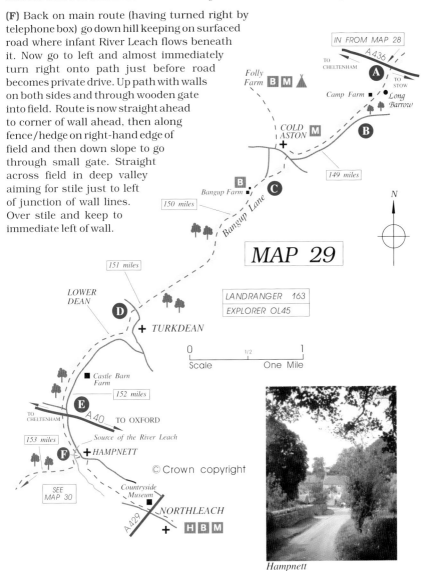

IN FROM MAP 28

A436

TO CHELTENHAM

TO STOW

A

Folly Farm **B M** ⛺

Camp Farm ■

● Long Barrow

B

COLD ASTON **M**
✝

149 miles

Bangup Farm **B** ■
C

150 miles

Bangup Lane

N

MAP 29

151 miles

LOWER DEAN

D

✝ TURKDEAN

LANDRANGER 163

EXPLORER OL45

0   1/2   1
Scale   One Mile

■ Castle Barn Farm

152 miles

E

TO CHELTENHAM

A40   TO OXFORD

153 miles

Source of the River Leach

F ✝ HAMPNETT

© Crown copyright

SEE MAP 30

Countryside Museum ■

A429

NORTHLEACH

✝ **H B M**

Hampnett

69

(A) Through wooden gate and go across busy minor road onto smaller road forking right (SP - *Fossebridge*). After about 50 yards turn right through double wooden gates down track with mature plantation on right and young plantation on left. Turn left at end of young plantation and note stone leaning against wall on immediate left beyond bend in wall. *This is known locally as the Hangman's Stone, and it appears to have been named as such due to a sheep-stealer who accidentally hung himself while getting over a stile in this wall with a stolen sheep in his arms. A highly moral, but rather unlikely story!* Now go into field through double wooden gates keeping to immediate left of another young plantation on its right. Down field now keeping to immediate left of hedge and fence, soon veering slightly right and passing beneath electric power-line with large pylon just to right. Through gap in fence coming in from left into smaller field with large barns of Oxpens Farm on left. Soon turn left with fence and wall to immediate right and, just before reaching barns, after stone wall, turn right through gate. Follow down between wall on right and fence with spinney on left. Go diagonally left across very small field.

(B) Soon turn right through gate onto well surfaced farm road and follow this down into valley. Cross stream, a tributary of River Coln and pass old, stone-lined sheep wash on right. Climb track up into farmyard, which marks our entry into Yanworth. Bend left and then right, following track through farmyard past attractive stone barns and, on right, delightful little Yanworth Church. *Here will be found a Norman south doorway, a chancel arch of the same period and a wall-painting of Old Father Time complete with his scythe.* Up surfaced road beyond church, turn left at top and almost immediately right onto road in village (SP - *Roman Villa*). Go through village, passing village hall on right, cast-iron water pump on left and delightful *Dolls' Cottage* and telephone box, both on right.

(C) Turn left at road junction (SP - *Fossebridge*) and go down road towards beautifully wooded Coln Valley. *Good view of fine Elizabethan mansion of Stowell Park well over to left.* Pass converted Yanworth Mill on right and, immediately beyond bridge over River Coln, turn right where road bends to left. Now on broad surfaced track with extensive woodlands up to left and water meadows to right as we walk parallel with River Coln. Many pheasants in woods - please keep dogs on lead.

(D) After one mile pass cottage on left and after another 200 yards go through gate to turn left onto surfaced road (SP - *Roman Villa*). Up fairly steep slope, keeping on surfaced road and ignoring track to left. Soon pass the National Trust's Chedworth Roman Villa on right and go onto footpath to immediate left of National Trust

reception building. *In an attractive woodland setting and dating from between AD 180 and AD 350, these very interesting and beautifully preserved remains include bath suites, a hypocaust and mosaic pavements. There is also a museum and shop, and a 9-minute introductory film provides a fascinating insight into life and work in the Romano-British countryside. Don't miss a visit here - you could even reward yourself with an ice cream!* Go

At Chedworth Roman Villa

up steep, stony path through woods, soon disregarding steps up to left and going through underbridge beneath old railway embankment. After 200 yards, turn left at x-rds of tracks and continue to climb up through woods. Straight, not right at junction of tracks, going onto possibly muddier track. Fork right at Y-junction of tracks going gently up hill.

(E) Over stile at end of wood and head straight across field to go to immediate right of fence coming in from left. Continue with fence now on immediate left, soon cross line of bridleway and through metal gate below sycamore tree. Go straight, not left, at next junction of paths and go steeply down through wood, initially on steps. Over stile at end of wood and keep in same direction across field in broad valley. Well concealed railway cutting beyond dense bushes to left, at southern end of old railway tunnel. Bear right just before cottage and go over stile onto surfaced road at entry to

Woods beyond Chedworth Roman Villa

Chedworth village. Soon pass church on right. *This light and airy building was considerably enriched in the Perpendicular period and has a stout Norman font, and, in contrast, an elegant 15th-century stone pulpit.* Keep on higher road (but bear left down path if you wish to visit the Seven Tuns, a welcoming inn with a spring bubbling out of a wall opposite). Pass attractive house and barn on right with pool in garden.

(F) Over first road and bear left up slope to left of village notice board. Immediately bear right across second road to go straight up track overhung with trees. After 300 yards, go straight over road onto track (SP -*Setts Farm House only*).

MAP 30

To Withington 2 miles
B **M**

Chedworth Roman Villa

Disused Railway Line

154 miles

The Hangman's Stone

Old Sheep Wash

Oxpens Farm

A IN FROM MAP 29

YANWORTH Village Hall

B

N

River Coln

C

155 miles

Stream

D

Yanworth Mill

157 miles

Old Railway Tunnel

156 miles

Stowell Park

E

LANDRANGER 163
EXPLORER OL45

F CHEDWORTH **B** **M**
Seven Tuns Inn

0   1/2   1
Scale   One Mile

SEE MAP 31

© Crown copyright

71

(A) At Setts Farm House keep on track through double wooden gates, then through two single gates and stay on this with open views ahead. Pass end of hedgeline on left and bear slightly left along track, with view ahead of 'restored' World War I airfield, known as 'RFC Rendcomb' (Strictly private - do not try to visit). Through wide gap in wall now following hedge on left and dropping gently into shallow valley. After about 200 yards, keep on track, leaving theoretical right-of-way and onto permissive section (not signed as such). Bear right in bottom of valley, keeping on track and soon turn left at junction of tracks ignoring tree-lined track ahead.

(B) After about 300 yards turn right at junction of tracks, leaving permissive section and re-join right-of-way. Keep along broad track with open field on both

sides, gradually rising out of valley. Through gap at end of track and turn left onto road which follows course of minor Roman road known as the White Way. Cross this road onto small lane to left of waymark to Greenmeadow Farm. Follow lane passing narrow strip of wood to left. Fine views of Rendcomb ahead including its 'chateau-style' stable-block tower. Down lane and up short, steep hill.

(C) Soon pass footpath to left. *Use this if you wish to divert to Cirencester down Churn Valley - five-and-a-half miles - using Map 31A. From Cirencester, use Map 31B to re-join the main route at the Tunnel House Inn (see Map 32, Point H) - a further three-and three-quarter miles). There would therefore be no extra mileage involved, as the total distance of this major diversion is the same as that between its starting and finishing points on the main route.* Back on main

A hint of France at Rendcomb

route just before entry to Rendcomb - turn left at road junction (phone box on left) by entry to estate village of Rendcomb, with Italianate Rendcomb Court used as boarding school. Pass Post Office shop and 'French-chateau-style' stable block (now school science building). Follow road to left. (But turn right if you wish to visit church.) *This was built by prosperous wool merchant, Sir Edmund Thame, son of the builder of better known Fairford church, with which it shares certain similarities. It also has a splendid Norman font.* Follow road down hill, under bridge, cross infant River Churn and pass Rendcomb Surgery before reaching busy A435.

(D) Cross A435 with great care, going right and almost immediately left onto lane (SP - *Unsuitable for Long Vehicles*). Go up lane for at least half-a-mile, looking back for good view of Rendcomb College. Go left through large wooden gate opposite cottage named *The Lodge* and just before large pylon. Go diagonally across field heading for left-hand end of dutch barn. Go through metal gate to immediate left of dutch barn and follow short fence on right before passing cottage. Immediately beyond cottage go over stile to right. Follow track to road into quiet hamlet of Woodmancote.

(E) Go left onto road in Woodmancote, telephone box soon on right by road junction. Bear right off road just beyond semi-detached house ('*No 2*') on right and before sign *North Cerney* and onto short, sunken bridleway. At end of this go slightly left across junction of surfaced drives, and then bear slightly right to go down lane passing just to right of Moor Wood, a large house with impressive gardens on both sides of lane.

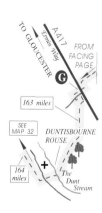

Keep on surfaced lane bearing slightly right to pass house with stables on both sides of lane and cartshed just beyond on right. Continue onto track with wood and stream on right.

(F) Soon fork left on track with hedge on left. Bend to left at valley bottom and climb up track to pass coniferous wood on left. After one-third-of-a-mile, at end of track, go straight ahead on concrete drive towards house near Dartley Farm,

Duntisbourne Rouse Church (see page 78)

but just before house go left onto tarmac lane leading to embanked A417 dual carriageway (*This follows the course of the Romans' Ermin Way, which ran from Silchester, near Reading, through Cirencester, to their legionary fortress at Gloucester*).

(G) Continue round to left where farm road becomes concreted and go through wooden gates. Turn right, onto minor road and under two bridges beneath A417. About 150 paces beyond 2nd bridge, turn sharp left, through small wooden gate to go back on yourself along farm road between wooden fences. Soon bear right to go parallel with A417 and at end of track turn right

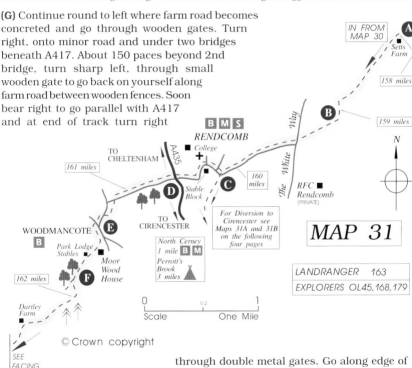

IN FROM MAP 30 **A**
Setts Farm
158 miles
B
159 miles
N
B M S
RENDCOMB
College
TO CHELTENHAM
A435
161 miles
160 miles
C
The White Way
RFC Rendcomb (PRIVATE)
Stable Block
D
TO CIRENCESTER
For Diversion to Cirencester see Maps 31A and 31B on the following four pages
MAP 31
WOODMANCOTE **E**
B
Park Lodge Stables
Moor Wood House
North Cerney
1 mile **B M**
Perrott's Brook
3 miles
162 miles **F**
LANDRANGER 163
EXPLORERS OL45,168,179
Dartley Farm
0 ... 1/2 ... 1
Scale   One Mile
© Crown copyright

SEE FACING PAGE

through double metal gates. Go along edge of field with hedge on left for about 100 yards before turning left through metal gate. Now go immediately right with bushy hedge now on right, then ignore opening on right and, after a while, through next metal gate still keeping hedge on right. Cirencester Park woodlands visible on horizon ahead. Continue skirting right-hand edge of field before bearing off right, out of field at bottom corner to go down path between hedge on right and wood on left. Continue down sunken lane and go over small bridge to left of ford crossing the Dunt stream in attractive Duntisbourne Rouse hamlet. (Now turn to page 78)

(A) Leave Main Route at Map 31 Point C, by turning left off road at top of slope just before entering Rendcomb. (No waymarks until we rejoin main route.) Go along top of field with fence to immediate right, keep in same line beyond fence'e end and through iron kissing gate. Continue at same angle across track and go down into narrow wood. Soon through possibly delapidated kissing gate, turn left into field and follow round it keeping fenced edge of wood on immediate left. Over stile, cross main track and go through small coniferous plantation to hunting gate into field, ignoring footpath sign up to left. Walk along pleasant meadow parallel with River Churn to right. At end of field, ignore footbridge to right, and go

In Baunton Churchyard

through hunting gate just beyond. Along winding track through next field with meandering Churn to right. Near end of field through gateway gap in wall over to left and bear half-left up track. Bear half-right up track onto well defined track and follow along top of steep slope coming up from right. Aim towards Cedar of Lebanon beyond house ahead and soon through large wooden gate at entry to North Cerney.

(B) Turn left onto road by phone box and immediately fork right (SP - *Calmsden*) *(but turn right if you wish to visit Bathurst Arms or church)*. Bear right up hill and almost immediately turn right off road and through wooden gate by transformer on poles. After a few yards turn left over stile and continue in same direction with fence on immediate right. Through squeeze stile beside hunting gate and follow to immediate left of fence beyond farm on right. Through large wooden gate into next field and follow right-hand edge of field with fence to right. Ignore bridge to right and through hunting gate, keeping to bottom of field with line of willows to right. Through large wooden gate and onto track with fence on left and hedge on right. Onto surfaced driveway at Perrott's Brook Farm with houses first on right and then on left. Keep straight down driveway passing barns on left and then bear right onto road.

(C) At road junction go straight across road and bear left onto track in woodland

carpeted with bluebells and other small flowers in spring *(but turn right if you wish to visit the Bear Inn - 200 yards, just across A435)*. Leave wood soon passing small building and follow track along right-hand edge of field. Through wooden gate and continue across meadow in same direction. Passing beneath bypass viaduct. Where

The Roman Amphitheatre, Cirencester (see page 76)

meadow narrows, bear

slightly left up path onto bank to keep in same direction through scrubby area. Through wooden gate and metal gate and onto track with beech hedge to left and small stream to right.

(D) Bear left at junction of tracks and onto surfaced road at entry to Baunton. Pass Baunton church on right. *Do try to visit this, to look at the unique 14th-century wall-painting of St Christopher.* Go straight across at road junction in Baunton, pass phone box on left and go round to right at T-junction. Bear left off road by tiny village green, onto surfaced track and soon through metal gate and then over stile by wooden gate. Follow well defined footpath across large field aiming for centre of wood ahead. Over small stile and up short, steep path into wood. Soon bear right onto well-defined path along woodland slope before bearing up left to go over stile at end of wood. Across field aiming for power pole to left of tower of Cirencester Church. At end of field, follow footpath waymark along field to go over stone stile beyond.

(E) Through metal gate just before Bowling Green Farm and keep onto surfaced roadway into outskirts of Cirencester passing house on left called 'The Old Dairy'. Keep straight along Bowling Green Lane to go over Cirencester's inner bypass with very great care. Pass phone box on left, over small bridge crossing River Churn and go straight ahead to T-junction. Turn left into Gloucester Street by the Nelson Inn. Over x-rds into Dollar Street *(but turn left if you wish to look at arcading of St John's Hospital - founded by Henry II).*

(F) Pass north side of Cirencester Parish Church on left and bear left into Market Place beyond church's west end.

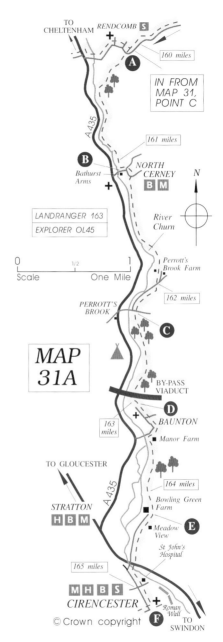

TO CHELTENHAM   RENDCOMB **S**

160 miles

A

IN FROM MAP 31, POINT C

A.435

161 miles

B
Bathurst Arms

NORTH CERNEY
B M

N

LANDRANGER 163
EXPLORER OL45

River Churn

0   1/2   1
Scale   One Mile

Perrott's Brook Farm

162 miles

PERROTT'S BROOK

C

MAP 31A

BY-PASS VIADUCT

D

163 miles

BAUNTON

Manor Farm

TO GLOUCESTER

A.435

164 miles

Bowling Green Farm

STRATTON
H B M

Meadow View

E

St John's Hospital

165 miles

M H B S
CIRENCESTER

© Crown copyright

Roman Wall

F   TO SWINDON

75

The busy market town of Cirencester stands on the site of Corinium Dobunnorum and was, for a time, Roman Britain's second largest city and meeting point of three major Roman roads. It remains today the undisputed centre of life and work in the southern Cotswolds and offers all that the Macmillan Way user requires in the way of shops, B&Bs, hotels, eating places and helpful TIC. Near our entry to the town are the surviving arcades of St John's Hospital, but most visitors will head for the Market Place, which is overlooked by Cirencester's fine Parish Church. This was generously endowed with the wealth of the town's wool merchants and has a magnificent Perpendicular tower, a massive three-storeyed south porch and an equally impressive interior. The turf-covered Roman amphitheatre lies to the south of the ring road and on the other side of the town there is a stretch of Roman city wall to the east of the delightful Abbey Grounds. The fascinating Corinium Museum has one of Britain's best collections of Romano-British material and is well worth visiting. To the right of our route out of the town lies the great expanse of Cirencester Park, with its Broad Ride stretching westwards to Sapperton, almost five miles away.

(A) Head southwards from the Market Place, go along Castle Street and over road at end onto Fosse Way. Head out of town on Fosse Way passing Bridges Garage on left and going over Stroud Road with great care by large roundabout onto A429. After 350 yards turn right off road beyond house on right opposite haulage depot and onto footpath going diagonally left across field with young trees. On reaching hedgeline bear left up track and keep to immediate right of all-weather games pitch. Follow tarmac path, pass sports pavilion on right and cross main drive to Royal Agricultural College (up to right).

Keep to left-hand edge of playing field, through squeeze stile to right of wooden gate and down grassy track with hedges on both sides. Through squeeze stile to left of wooden gate and down track in same direction (track up to left leads to College Farm).

Straight, not right, at junction of tracks in valley. Out of valley on grassy track and beyond farm buildings and house on left (Field Barn) bear right onto surfaced track with fence to left. After 200 yards turn left over stile by beech tree and follow left-hand edge of field. Turn right in first corner of field and keep to left-hand edge of field with woodland to left. Through gate just to right of field corner and keep in same direction down left-hand edge of next field.

(B) Through two metal gates crossing narrow belt of woodland and keep in same direction along left-hand edge of next field, eventually passing pool beyond hedge to left. Handsome 18th-century Bledisloe Lodge visible over to right. Over stile on left and turn right to continue in same direction within very narrow, young plantation. Pass Fosse Hill Lodge on left and soon cross minor road and over stile in stone wall. Follow down two fields with fence to immediate left with

Cirencester Church

The Tunnel House Inn, near Coates

parkland of Trewsbury House up to left within earth-works of large Iron Age hill fort (not very apparent). Over stile and keep in same line but now with fence to right.

(C) Through metal gate, turn left onto track over old canal bridge and immediately turn right to go onto towpath to left of overgrown canal bed - the remains of the Thames and Severn Canal *(see page 80)*. *(But turn right again, go under bridge and along towpath for half a mile if you wish to visit Thames Head - the official and often dry, source of the River Thames - and possibly link to head of Thames Path (see page 80)).* After half a mile, go under railway bridge and pass ruined 18th-century Gothick canal round house. After 400 yards, go under road bridge and continue along towpath, now beside a water-filled section of canal to arrive at southern portal of canal tunnel and Tunnel House Inn, thereby rejoining main route at Map 32, Point H (page 79).

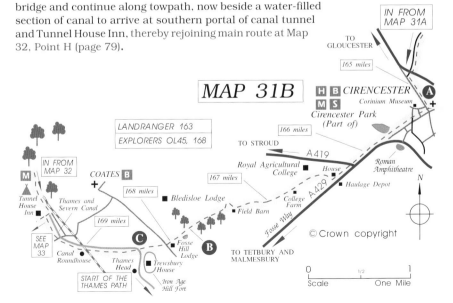

(A) Go up short lane and turn right onto minor road (SP - *The Duntisbournes / Youth Hostel*). After 100 yards pass entry to exceptionally interesting Duntisbourne Rouse church on right - don't miss a visit. *This tiny Saxon church has a saddleback roof to its tower and an interior complete with box pews, carved misericords to its choir stalls and medieval wall paintings on its north chancel wall. Being built on a slope it has, most unusually, a little crypt beneath its eastern end.* After about 300 yards turn left onto bridleway. Go along bridleway and after 300 yards bear right by wooden barn on left and follow track to right.

(B) After three-quarters-of-a-mile, cross minor road and through wooden gate onto further bridleway, which skirts to right (north) of Overley Wood - the northern fringe of Cirencester Park's great woodlands. *Please note that almost all the way from here to the Tunnel House Inn (see opposite) is within Cirencester Park, part of the Bathurst Estate, and to meet this estate's requirements, Macmillan Way waymarks will unfortunately not be displayed. However, the route is well signed with standard waymarks and little difficulty should be experienced.* At end of bridleway turn left onto minor road and pass Gloucester Lodge on left - this is one of the northern entrances to Cirencester Park. Continue southwards on minor road.

(C) Immediately after passing signed entrance to Pinbury Park (private) turn right onto bridleway and immediately right again through hunting gate. Follow an indistinct path on immediate right of hawthorn hedge and parallel with private road to Pinbury Park on right. Where hedge and drive turn left veer away from hedge down towards drive. Soon leave private road and skirt to left of pond, going between pond and its feeding spring. Through double gates just beyond pond and follow field path south-westwards aiming between two power-poles. *Lovely 17th-century Pinbury Park (house) visible back across valley to right.*

(D) Through gate into bushy area and at junction of tracks just beyond, carry straight ahead, slightly up hill, ignoring path to left. Continue south-westwards on path in middle of delightful meadow ringed by fine trees. Through gate keeping on path to left of fence with view of house called *The Leasowes* to right. Continue up path and turn right onto well defined bridleway (Signed - *Permissive*). Through gate and bear half-left to cross field to telephone box in Sapperton village. *Sapperton church is over to right and is approached down a path below yew trees. In the north transept of this largely 18th-century building, Sir Henry Poole, who died in 1616, lies in a great canopied Renaissance tomb, with many effigies. Adjacent to it is another Poole tomb dated 1574. In the south transept Sir Robert Atkyns, who died in 1711, lies on his left elbow with his hand resting upon a book. He was the county historian and wrote 'The Ancient and Present State of Gloucestershire'. Trim and colourful Sapperton is very much a Bathurst estate village and below it runs the two-and-a-quarter-mile-long tunnel of the Thames and Severn Canal (see page 80), the western portal of which is at Daneway in the valley below Sapperton.*

Sapperton Church

(E) Back on main route - turn left up hill near telephone box, soon passing the Bell Inn on left and bus stop. Turn right at road junction (SP - *Cherington*) and soon cross 'The Sapperton Broad Avenue', *a broad grassy ride, also known as 'The Broad Ride', which runs eastwards for nearly five miles to Cirencester, with only a short break in open country around Pope's Seat. A notice states 'You are welcome on horseback or on foot along the Sapperton Broad*

Avenue. Please keep dogs on leads'. It should be noted however that this facility applies only between 8 am and 5pm.

(F) Soon turn left at x-rds (SP - *Cirencester*). Go along road, with view to right of one of the spoil heaps created by the excavators of the tunnel for the Thames and Severn Canal. Ignore first fingerpost to right and proceed with great care along this often busy minor road until a plantation joins our road on left. At this point turn right, off road and through gap in stone wall. Cross field, through large metal gates and cross busy A419 with great care to go through more large metal gates. Keep in same direction across field noting another tunnel spoil heap over to right.

(G) At end of field go through gate into Hailey Wood and continue ahead veering slightly left on track to plunge into this very large wood. Continue on track ignoring other crossing rides and paths and approximately following the course of canal tunnel beneath. *Note spoil heap to right (not easy to spot in summer) with exposed air shaft, but keep away from fenced edge - it could be very dangerous. Like the rest, this shaft was first used to extract spoil from the tunnel beneath and was then used for ventilation.* After about 500 yards veer slightly to left and soon go straight across wide track which descends from estate saw-mill up to left (not visible) and which also goes to right, over embankment, with parapet of railway bridge just visible beyond. Continue on footpath, then turn half-right at junction with track coming in from left. Go under railway line, turn left and follow path running parallel with railway, and pass through gate before reaching vicinity of Tunnel House Inn.

(H) Turn right into inn car parking area. We are joined here by the alternative route from Rendcomb via Cirencester (see end of page 77.)

Duntisbourne Abbots 2 miles **B**

MIDDLE DUNTISBOURNE **B**

164 miles

DUNTISBOURNE ROUSE

165 miles **B**

A   IN FROM MAP 31

Gloucester Lodge

Overley Wood

166 miles   **C**

MAP 32

Pinbury Park

Pond

LANDRANGER 163

EXPLORERS 168,179

D

The Leasowes

167 miles

0   1/2   1
Scale   One Mile

Daneway 1 mile **M**   **E**

SAPPERTON **M**

Cirencester

N

Frampton Mansell 2 miles **M B**   **F**

The Broad Ride

168 miles

Park

(part of)

Course of Thames and Severn Canal Tunnel

A419

TO STROUD   **G**   TO CIRENCESTER

© Crown copyright

Ventilation Shafts   Saw Mill

Hailey

169 miles

Wood

H   Canal Tunnel Entrance

For Diversion from Cirencester, see Maps 31A & 31B

M The Tunnel House Inn

SEE MAP 33

For link to Thames Path - see Map 33

79

(A) Go into car parking area in front of Tunnel House Inn and then between inn and low building to its left, passing old cider press on left, going down to gap in wall. *(However, follow towpath along bank of partly restored Thames and Severn Canal if you wish to link onto the Thames Path at Thames Head, the source of the Thames, which is about a mile away.) The Tunnel House Inn was built to house, feed and especially water, the navvies who dug the canal tunnel and the thirsty boatmen who used it when completed. The tunnel, the delightful portal of which is still visible near the inn, was completed in 1789. It enabled boats to cross the Cotswolds from the head of the navigable Thames at Lechlade to the Severn via the Stroudwater Canal. It was abandoned in 1927, but there is now an ambitious 10-year plan to re-open it. Now an attractive and welcoming pub, the Tunnel House is full of curiosities and delights. Don't miss a call here - it's a great pub.*

(B) Now back on main route beyond Tunnel House Inn, having gone through gap in wall beyond cider press. Go along wide footpath bearing slightly right, across field, *with very slight earthworks of Roman 'settlement' sometimes visible over to left. Now known as Tunnel Mouth Camp it was probably a religious complex dating from the 3rd or 4th century AD, but it has never been systematically excavated (Do not trespass).* Over stone stile in wall into next field and now follow line of power-poles, which presently leads towards stile in cross-wall ahead between 3rd and 4th poles. Over this stile and up across next field still following poles to go through small gate beside stile. Go diagonally right between two large sycamores, across field to fingerpost and through metal gate near small house in Tarlton.

(C) At entry to Tarlton, *a minute village with a number of pleasant houses and a small neo-Norman church,* go slightly left, cross road and turn right onto well surfaced track between high stone walls, leading through farmyard. Pass converted barns on right and farm buildings on left to leave Tarlton on track beyond farm cottages on right. Bear slightly left keeping on farm track and after about half-a-mile, at end of track, go through metal gate into field. Turn half right to cross corner of field and through second metal gate. Keep in same direction across corner of next field to go through third metal gate and across larger field aiming to right of tall trees in line of woodland ahead. Go through wooden gate into scrubby woodland. Now veer slightly left to follow very short grassy track.

(D) Soon turn left onto semi-surfaced track and head south-westwards with woodlands to left. After about 600 yards go straight ahead to join minor road. After 50 yards go straight ahead onto track where road turns left. After just over half a mile cross minor road and through opening onto further track in same direction.

(E) After about 350 yards and at first wall-line to right, just before end of field, turn right through old, small gateway *(now on permissive path - Macmillan Way walkers only)* and go up right-hand side of field keeping hedge and wall on immediate right. At end of field bear slightly right through gap and bear slightly left joining farm track. Drop down on track bearing left at bottom with good view of delightful Hazleton Manor over to left. Bear left at junction of tracks and keep on track out of small valley (do not go

80

East portal of the Thames and Severn Canal tunnel

through gates into field to right). Now bear right onto concrete track, then left, with converted barns to left. Turn right just beyond transformer on poles to left *(re-joining normal right-of-way)* and go straight along farm road to Shepherd's Cottages.

(F) At end of farm road go straight across field to gate. Through this gate into wood and after about 50 yards, fork right along waymarked pathway (probably red arrows and dots). Soon bear left and after going along narrow path, emerge at end of wood. Now follow right-hand field boundaries to gate in corner. Cross between two power poles to indistinct gap in hedge. Go along three more fields in a straight line, passing Field Barn on left and keeping to immediate left of hedgelines where they exist.

(G) Through gap beside metal gate, bear right onto public road and go straight, not right by Coxe's Farm at entry to Cherington village (SP - Avening). Turn right (SP - Avening) by wide green *overlooked by several pleasant 18th and early 19th-century cottages, with an ancient wellhead on it, inscribed, 'Let Him that is athirst, come'. The nearby church is largely 13th-century in origin and has a Norman south doorway with tympanum and a Norman tub font.* Just beyond village, go over diagonal x-rds roads on hill (SP - Stroud) and go down steep hill with care. At bottom of hill bear left off road through parking space and through wooden gate. Keep on often muddy path with stream on right and then pass delightful lake on right, known as Cherington Pond. At end of lake bear left up slight incline.

(H) Soon through small wooden gate and bear right onto minor road. Keep on road through hamlet of Nag's Head (the pub has gone long ago), keeping straight, not right by telephone box. After 500 yards go straight, not left and after further 300 yards, turn left onto busier road into Avening village.

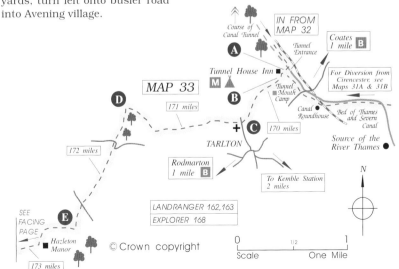

(A) After 200 yards pass Cross Inn on left and go straight onto B4014 (SP - *Nailsworth*), passing small general stores on left. After 200 yards bear left up Point Road by telephone box. Soon keep straight, **not** left up Pound Hill, but descend, with glimpse of Avening church down to right and then bear left at T-junction and up hill, still on Point Road. Straight, not left at road junction by de-restriction signs (SP - *West End*) and just beyond, turn left through large wooden gate opposite Church Farm Barn, up a steep grassy footpath. Over stile (good views back over valley to Gatcombe Park) and walk as near as possible to right-hand edge of field. Keep to right of small spinney near right-hand edge of field and over stone stile. Follow wall to left soon passing fine farmhouse on left with clock tower.

(B) Over stile to left of metal gate, cross surfaced farm drive, then over stile and along next field keeping wall on left. Over rudimentary stile and continue with wall still on left, but just before end of field, bear left over massive stone stile and go diagonally left across field aiming for far left-hand corner just to right of clump of trees. Go through gap, turn left through second gap and immediately right onto B4014 road. Go along road with great care and after 250 yards, at first gentle bend to left, bear right through gap just after two power poles into young plantation. Go round to left of plantation and, at the field, go diagonally right aiming just to left of pylon to corner of field. Over stone stile, cross minor road and through gap in wall. Go diagonally right, across field aiming for line of trees at far side. Through large gap in cross-hedge and into next field keeping to immediate right of parallel wall. Over stile in left-hand end of wire cross-fence near end of field.

(C) Soon go through gate to cross minor road. *(But walk about 200 yards down road to left for glimpse of Chavenage House through its entrance gates.) Chavenage is a delightful Elizabethan manor house, which was once visited by Oliver Cromwell, to persuade the owner, Colonel Nathaniel Stephens, to put his name to Charles I's Death Warrant. The colonel grudgingly agreed, but then died within three months of the king's execution, apparently full of remorse.*

(C) On main route - over road going slightly right, onto farm road with asbestos barn to right and old stone barn to left. Bear slightly left down sometimes muddy bridleway (known as Chavenage Lane) going between walls, soon passing wood on left, rich with bluebells in late spring. At end of wood, go down bridleway bordered by hedges and trees.

(D) Through gate, bear down left and through another gate into bottom of small valley. *If you wish to divert to Tetbury for overnight stop, fork left onto path along valley (probably not waymarked) keeping low wall on left. Bear left over stile at end of wall and along often muddy, ill-defined path in wooded area. Keep parallel with*

field on right. Turn right onto lane and in a few yards bear left at road junction. Soon enter Tetbury - under two miles. This unspoilt little market town is centred upon its delightful 17th-century Market House and the nearby church of St Mary. But in addition to these main features, Tetbury has a wealth of interesting old buildings and is well worth visiting. To return to main route - leave town centre on Church Street, turn right into West Street, opposite church and then bear left down Cotton's Lane. Soon turn left onto Cutwell and cross River Avon on small stone bridge beside ford. Turn right onto Longfurlong Lane and leave town on this, keeping straight not right well beyond. At end of Longfurlong Lane, go through two gates in front of Elmestree Lodge. Now go diagonally left across fields and parkland in front of Elmestree House

Autumn at Westonbirt
(see page 84)

following waymarks. Slight hint of Highgrove House over to left. Then into another field with hedge on left before going on grassy gallop for short distance. Then bear left over stile through hedge and follow in same direction along three fields, keeping to immediate left of hedge-line. Now over final stile and re-join main route at Point G (see below) by turning left onto Hookshouse Lane, some 400 yards north of diagonal x-rds near Westonbirt. (Distance from Tetbury under three miles)

(D) Back on main route, in valley beyond Chavenage. Aim slightly left and go up slope with fence and bushes to right, with good view back to Chavenage House. Through large metal gate at top of slope and continue on bridleway with hedge to right. Fine distant views to left of Tetbury with its splendid, tall-spired church. Continue on bridleway with good views of Beverston Castle over to right before reaching A4135.

(E) Turn right onto often busy A4135 and almost immediately turn left off it through hunting gate beside large wooden gates. *(But follow road westwards for half-a-mile if you wish to visit Beverston. The church in this small village has an unusual Anglo-Saxon sculpture on its tower and some interesting features within. Beverston Castle, one of the few surviving Cotswold castles, is nearby, a largely 13th-century building with 17th-century additions. It is not open but glimpses can be obtained from the road.)* On main route - follow broad and grassy track, eventually going through gate onto more defined track with trees and fences on both sides, and into small valley. Up track beyond it and along left of field before going through gate and bearing right at Hookshouse hamlet.

(F) Almost immediately fork left at road junction by Hookshouse Pottery on right (SP - Westonbirt). Follow Hookshouse Lane southwards passing Charlton Down (house) on left.

(G) After about half-a-mile pass footpath sign on left (this is where diversion route from Tetbury rejoins main route). Distant view to right of pavilion of the Beaufort Polo Club.

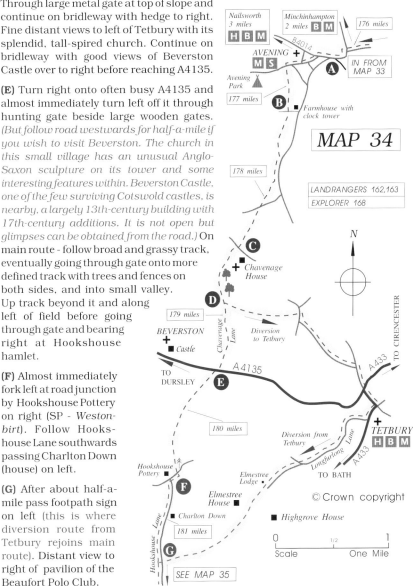

Nailsworth 3 miles **H B M**

Minchinhampton 2 miles **B M**

176 miles

B4014

AVENING **M S**

IN FROM MAP 33

Avening Park

177 miles **B**

Farmhouse with clock tower

MAP 34

LANDRANGERS 162,163

EXPLORER 168

178 miles

N

C

Chavenage House

D

179 miles

BEVERSTON

Castle

Chavenage Lane

Diversion to Tetbury

TO CIRENCESTER

A4135

A433

TO DURSLEY

E

180 miles

Diversion from Tetbury

TETBURY **H B M**

Longfurlong Lane

A433

TO BATH

Hookshouse Pottery

F

Elmestree Lodge

© Crown copyright

Elmestree House

Charlton Down

181 miles

Highgrove House

Hookshouse Lane

G

SEE MAP 35

0   1/2   1
Scale   One Mile

(A) At diagonal x-rds turn right over stile and along field with wall on immediate right. Through gate and keep to left-hand edge of field with northern edge of Westonbirt Arboretum to left - occasional vistas of tall and exotic trees, undulating lawns, leisurely seats and arbours. Through gate into next field, still following wall on left. Down Farm visible over to right with the Beaufort Polo Club's pavilion to its immediate right. Through offset gap in wooden fence and through two more gates continuing on same line.

(B) Just before spinney, visible ahead, go through gate on left into Arboretum's field. Descend this field on sunken cart track, then veer slightly right in small valley and go over squeeze stile (ignoring standard waymarks) on edge of wood (now on a Permissive Path). *But turn left down valley and purchase entry tickets at far end of car park if you wish to leave course of Macmillan Way and visit rest of Arboretum, with its Visitor Centre, cafe and shop.) Westonbirt Arboretum was the creation of Sir Robert Holford, the owner of nearby neo-Elizabethan Westonbirt House, which is now a school. This world famous collection of over 13,000 trees stands in a beautiful 600-acre landscape with woodland paths and grassy glades. It has been owned by the Forestry Commission since 1956.* Back on main route - over squeeze stile into Westonbirt Arboretum's Silk Wood and bear slightly to right before going left up slope. At top of bank go over well defined path, bearing very slightly right, passing waymark post. Go along well defined grassy ride to next post beneath beech tree. Bear very slightly left aiming for next post and here, veer very slightly right to arrive at post beneath large pine tree. Here veer slightly left to head for next post where you turn 90 degrees left to follow path out of trees, down grassy slope to left of small clump of trees.

(C) At drive's junction keep in same direction down the Broad Drive, main north-south axis of the Silk Wood. Keep in same direction, ignoring paths to left and right and aiming for large gate in distance. Go through hunting gate beside large gate, which marks southern extremity of Silk Wood *(but turn right (SP - Willow Collection), along path just within wood for Avenue Farm, but only if you have booked B&B and obtained route directions)*. On main route, cross field keeping to left of hedge.

(D) Through metal gate, cross busy A433 with great care, passing from Gloucestershire into Wiltshire and going onto wide track (Wood Lane) between house on left and kennels on right (SP - *Knockdown Road*) (beware of dog droppings). Through gate into next field keeping hedge on immediate left. Tower of Sherston church already visible well ahead, with distant Marlborough Downs on skyline well to its left. Follow path to end of field and through gate to cross very narrow field with barn to right. Soon pass beneath ash trees and into next field keeping on track with hedge to immediate right.

(E) Through gate at end of field and continue in same direction down road. Soon pass Halfway Bush Farm on right and 500 yards beyond, go through gate on left at *Bridleway* sign. Go diagonally right, across field to far corner aiming for farm

buildings well beyond. Bear right in corner through metal gate and along left-hand edge of field with hedge and wall on left. Through gap in cross-hedge and continue in same line with hedge still on left. At end of field go straight ahead onto wide track with hedge on left and wall on right. Sherston visible over to right and house to left.

The Broad Drive, Westonbirt Arboretum

(F) Turn right onto road but immediately over stile (possibly difficult to spot) and cross field to kissing gate in wall with Sherston church tower visible ahead. Through kissing gate and follow well used path to another kissing gate. Up driveway with houses on right and wall on left at entry to Sherston and bear right onto B4040. *A large village with wide main street, Sherston was a borough by the 15th century and the variety of beautiful stone houses and inns still bear witness to its past prosperity. Only just over the border into Wiltshire, but it already seems to have a slightly 'West Country' flavour, with several inns offering food and a number of shops. Its church has a handsomely vaulted Perpendicular porch and a stout tower, surprisingly built as late as 1730.* Walk through Sherston on B4040, passing Carpenters Arms on left and church on right. Pass Rattlebone Inn on left, Post Office on right and phone box on left. Now take care when walking down steep road with dangerously blind bend.

(G) Soon cross infant River Avon *(this one flows into the Bristol Channel at Avonmouth)* and immediately beyond, go over stone stile on left (SP - *The Grove*). *In the event of flooding in field ahead, turnabout, soon fork right and take first four turns to right, to use minor roads to rejoin route near Convery Ciders - see below.* On main route - bear right beyond stile aiming for bridge in field. Over bridge crossing tributary of River Avon, continue in same direction with stream now on right into wooded area known as 'The Grove'. Through kissing gate and go straight across very small field dotted with scrub. Soon through another kissing gate and into large open terraced field. Go along terrace but before end of field veer up left just before power-pole and up onto top terrace to go over high stone stile in far corner. Veer slightly left and head for waymark post soon visible across field.

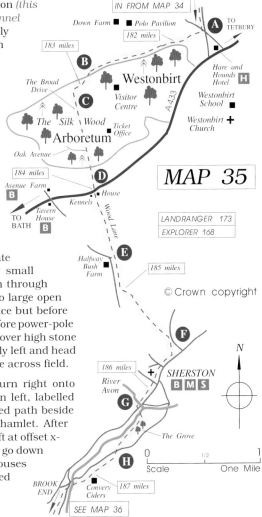

IN FROM MAP 34

Down Farm ■ ■ Polo Pavilion

182 miles

A TO TETBURY

183 miles

B

Westonbirt

Hare and Hounds Hotel **H**

The Broad Drive

C

Visitor Centre

A433

Westonbirt School ■

The Silk Wood

Ticket Office

Westonbirt ✝ Church

Arboretum

Oak Avenue

184 miles

D

Avenue Farm

B

■ House

Kennels

TO BATH

Tavern House

B

Wood Lane

MAP 35

LANDRANGER 173

EXPLORER 168

Halfway Bush Farm ■

E

185 miles

© Crown copyright

F

N

186 miles

River Avon

✝ SHERSTON **B M S**

G

The Grove

0   1/2   1

Scale   One Mile

H

BROOK END

Convery Ciders

187 miles

SEE MAP 36

(H) Over stile in wall and turn right onto road. Pass ornate postbox on left, labelled *Vineyard* and soon over raised path beside ford at entry to Brook End hamlet. After houses on both sides, turn left at offset x-rds (SP - *No Through Road*) to go down small lane with pleasant old houses on one side. Go along raised path beside another ford (on left) before going on gravel track.

(A) Bear up right towards stable yard at entry to Luckington, but just before entrance gates with small lions, go through gap in wall to their left and onto path through churchyard, keeping to right of church. *This is a modest building of 13th-century origin with some handsome 18th-century tomb chests in its churchyard. It has a delightful neighbour in Luckington Court, a mellow and beautifully proportioned Queen Anne house.* Through front gate of churchyard onto tarmac path leading to another gate onto road. Turn right onto road, immediately pass entrance to Luckington Court on right and after a few yards turn left and over stile onto path between two houses *(but go straight ahead up road if you wish to visit the Old Royal Ship Inn, or village shop).* Soon over stile into field, first following fence on right, then diagonally right to gap in hedge passing two houses on right. Now go left diagonally to far bottom corner of field. Over wooden stile and follow winding path down into more wooded area. Over bridge crossing stream and turn right to go along valley bottom, with willow-bordered stream now to right, and head for gate.

(B) Through gate, turn right onto minor road. Immediately before road junction, turn left off road and go over small stile (or through gap) in wall to left of gate. Go up grounds of house keeping close to wall on left and to left of two outbuildings. Through gate into small paddock and over stile into large field. Continue in same line (southwards) keeping to left-hand edge of field with hedge on left. Go through very wide gap in partial cross hedge.

(C) *(Follow these route directions with care.)* Now veer right (south-westwards) to aim well to right of ash tree in middle of facing hedge. Through waymarked gap in hedge to right of ash tree and continue in same direction, diagonally across next field aiming for far right-hand top corner. Keep to immediate left of small triangular plantation and near corner of field through stone squeeze-stile in small stone wall. Turn left along hedge and then straight across field aiming for waymarked stile in hedge. Over this stile and go across next field passing well to left of small pond (with Hebden Farm visible over to right) to go through large metal gate. Note old brick-kiln over to right just beyond small house.

(D) Bear left beyond gate (now southwards) aiming to left of bushes which surround a larger, partly concealed, pond. Over stile by gateway to left of pond and veer slightly right aiming for point between two oaks in valley. Soon over two small concrete 'bridges' and through underbridge in railway embankment carrying busy Swindon - Bristol line (Do not attempt to cross railway line, which is used by many very fast trains). Now head up towards lone oak tree in large meadow and then to right-hand end of wood on left.

Remains of Lugbury Long Barrow

(E) Through gateway at end of wood on left and veer slightly left aiming for gate just to left of woods ahead. Through gate, and veer left to cross small part of field aiming for gap which lies to left of sight-line to church tower ahead. Over stile in hedge and continue in same direction now aiming for gateway with house well beyond it. Through gateway and bear diagonally right across field towards gate in hedge ahead. Through gate, bear right onto road and soon bear left at road junction near entry to small village of Littleton Drew, which has no shop or inn. *Its church has a slender Perpendicular tower and in the porch are two large pieces of a 9th-century Saxon cross.* Go straight through village passing telephone box and church on right and ignoring footpath signs.

(F) Follow road out of village, going straight, not left at road junction just beyond and soon beneath noisy M4 motorway to arrive at T-junction. Cross busy B4039 with great care and go straight down narrow surfaced lane opposite (SP - *Bridleway*). Pass Goulter's Mill Farm on right (B & B), then bear left passing cart-shed on left before crossing bridge over By Brook *(we shall soon rejoin this stream and follow it until reaching Box - see page 90).* Bear left beyond bridge, through wooden gate and soon bear right, following track up hill to right of beech plantation. Through metal gate at end of plantation and keep straight up right-hand edge of field with wall to right. Through hunting gate at top of field and keep straight along right-hand edge of field with hedge on right. *Note Lugbury Long Barrow over to left, with the great stones of its main chambered tomb exposed on its top. Described by the 17th-century antiquary, John Aubrey, as 'a great Table stone of bastard freestone leaning on two pitched perpendicular stones', it is still impressive today. Constructed in Neolithic times it must already have been over two thousand years old when the Roman legionaries were building the nearby Fosse Way.* Bear right beyond small spinney and go through two metal hunting gates. Follow to immediate right of stone wall and after veering left, through large metal gate keeping on track to immediate right of wall.

(G) Through large metal gates and turn left onto road. Follow this road and over small x-rds crossing the Fosse Way (see page 66) (SP - *Nettleton Mill*). *(But turn right if you wish to visit Stables Tea Room or Fosse Farm Country Hotel - visible from here.)* Follow sunken lane, passing golf course on left, then over ladder stile beside gate and go quietly between houses at Nettleton Mill.

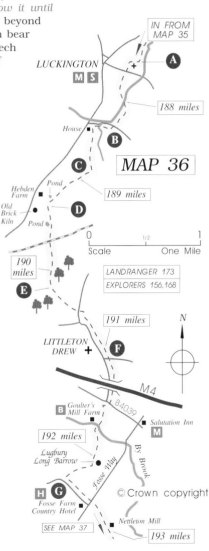

IN FROM MAP 35

A

LUCKINGTON
M S

188 miles

House

B

MAP 36

Hebden Farm — Pond

189 miles

Old Brick Kiln — Pond

C

D

0 — 1/2 — 1
Scale — One Mile

190 miles

LANDRANGER 173
EXPLORERS 156,168

E

191 miles

N

LITTLETON DREW

F

M4

B4039

Goulter's Mill Farm
B

Salutation Inn
M

192 miles

Lugbury Long Barrow

Fosse Way

By Brook

H G

Fosse Farm Country Hotel

Nettleton Mill

SEE MAP 37

193 miles

(A) Through concealed kissing gate to right of wrought-iron gate and bear left onto tree-shaded, surfaced path with pretty tributary stream alongside on left. Soon over stile and emerge onto golf course where we turn right and go on well surfaced path, keeping eye open for stray golf-balls and virtually silent golf-trolleys. Cross By

Houses near the Market Cross, Castle Combe

Brook over attractive neo-Gothic stone bridge and immediately turn right keeping on well surfaced path. *Manor House Hotel visible down valley to right.* At wooden gate fork left going slightly uphill, leave golf course and go up path, soon with wall on right and woods up to left. Turn right through squeeze-stile and down stone steps with walls on both sides. Under small stone bridge and soon onto surfaced driveway leading into Castle Combe.

(B) Under bridged gap between two houses. *This gap frames a delightful view of the Market Cross and the many old buildings surrounding it. Castle Combe lies snugly in the wooded valley of the little By Brook, with several fine old buildings around its little Market Cross reminding us of wealth once generated here by cloth weavers. The substantial tower of the largely Perpendicular church was built in 1434 'at the expense of the clothiers of the district', and the church's interior is well worth visiting.* Pass Castle Inn on left and church over to right before bearing right by Market Cross onto busier road with White Hart Inn opposite. Pass small gift shop on right. Over attractive stone bridge crossing By Brook. *It was in 1966 that the streamside down to the left was temporarily transformed by the producers of the film* Dr Doolittle *into a tiny 'harbour' complete with boats and jetty, a move not universally popular at the time.*

(C) Beyond end of village, turn left to cross small stone bridge over By Brook and immediately bear right onto well used path (SP - *Long Dean*). Over stone stile and bear up path to left into 'Conservation Area'. Now on slope with stream down to right, trees above to left and pools soon visible to right. Along path partly overhung with trees and bushes and into woodlands - fairly muddy in wet weather. Eventually go over stone stile across wall by gate and over another stile before starting to descend track with entry to sewage works on right (not very apparent).

(D) Enter pretty stone hamlet of Long Dean in its quiet, wooded valley, bearing right over small bridge and right again by Nut Tree Cottage up to left. Leave hamlet on track, ignore waymark to left, cross bridge over By Brook ignoring waymark to right. Bear right at end of track by last house in hamlet and up steep, sunken path through woods. Through gate at end of woods and keep on well defined path with overhanging hedge to immediate right. Good views across valley to left. At gap in bushes, where main path bears to right, fork left following well defined path across slope of field and aiming for woods at far left-hand top end. Over stile and turn left onto road. Follow this narrow sunken road with great care down hill through woodlands, keeping on left-hand side to be on outside of bend.

(E) Bear right onto busy A420 (SP - *Bristol*) at entry to village of Ford. Pass bus shelter on right. Almost immediately cross A420 with care and turn left onto minor road (SP - *Colerne*). Pass White Hart Inn on left, go straight, not left just beyond, and at end of village, beyond house called *Tredena* on right, turn left over stile. Go round field keeping fence and trees on immediate left with small stream soon joining By Brook. Now veer right keeping By Brook, with its fishermen's benches, on left. Bear left, over footbridge crossing attractive By Brook above weir and over stone stile immediately beyond. Bear left by end of weir, following path along foot of woods to left and after climbing a little, go straight ahead to gate in right-hand corner of field.. Through gate and go diagonally left to aim for gate in far left-hand corner of field.

(F) Through metal gate, go over road at T-junction and over stile almost opposite. Go to left of Slaughterford's churchyard wall. Pass gate to churchyard on right. *The church with its pleasant tower lay derelict for nearly 200 years, having apparently been greatly damaged by Cromwell's troops when on their way to Ireland. It was rebuilt in 1883 and its interior still has a Victorian flavour. The small village just beyond lies quietly in the deep, wooded valley of the By Brook.* Go straight down to gate beyond churchyard to bear left onto pathway above road. *The postbox here is one of only seven in the whole country of Edward VII vintage.* Pass village seat and attractive cottages on left. Bear left keeping on road with By Brook now on immediate right. Bear left onto narrow road just before bridge on right (SP - *Weight limit 7.5 tonnes*). Bear right keeping on road overhung with trees (ignoring footpath and bridleway fingerposts).

(G) Straight, not left, at road junction at end of woods and onto Weavern Lane which is surfaced in its initial stages. Go straight across keeping on lane (lane up to left leads to Honeybrook Farm). Weavern Lane now overhung with trees and often muddy. At start of Husseyhill Wood, with its attractive coppice plantations, go straight across at junction of tracks, ignoring waymark to left.

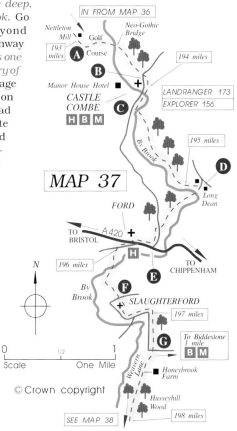

IN FROM MAP 36

Nettleton Mill

Golf Course

Neo-Gothic Bridge

193 miles

A

B

194 miles

Manor House Hotel

CASTLE COMBE

C

H B M

LANDRANGER 173

EXPLORER 156

By Brook

195 miles

D

Long Dean

MAP 37

FORD

TO BRISTOL

A 420

196 miles

H

E

TO CHIPPENHAM

N

By Brook

F

SLAUGHTERFORD

197 miles

G

To Biddestone 1 mile

B M

Honeybrook Farm

0   1/2   1
Scale   One Mile

Weavern Lane

© Crown copyright

Husseyhill Wood

198 miles

SEE MAP 38

(A) After about half-a-mile through woods turn left, keeping on track which soon becomes much narrower, with overhanging bushes. After 250 yards turn right off lane by oak trees and through metal gate. Go down narrow bridleway into more open country with hedge on right and fence on left. At end of field go down sunken path with hedge to left and fence to right. Through small wooden gate and down path with fence still on right. Cross track at end of short field, through small wooden gate and pass notice stating *'No swimming'*. Cross small stream with ruins of Weavern Farm over to right and fences on both sides of path.

(B) Over small bridge crossing now substantial By Brook and through small wooden gate going up slope. Along path with Tilley's Wood just to right and fence to left. *Pleasant views to left of By Brook and Hungerford Woods on slopes beyond.* Through small wooden gate, go left following well marked path across field with By Brook down to left and bushes and trees to right. Through small wooden gate to left of metal gate with By Brook just below to left. Go across field and eventually pass Widdenham Farmhouse on left before going over stile by large wooden gate on to surfaced driveway.

(C) Onto road passing Widdenham Farm's farmyard and cottages on right and soon go straight ahead through large metal gate where road goes to right. Cross large field following path running approximately parallel with By Brook. Through small gate with By Brook now on immediate left and through field with By Brook still on left, heading for metal gate with farmhouse just beyond.

(D) Over stile beside metal gate and bear left onto road passing Saltbox Farm on right (B&B). Bear right at road junction beyond Saltbox Farm and up slight incline before turning left to go over possibly half-hidden stile. Follow left-hand hedge for short distance, then through squeeze stile and bear right on well used path to cross large field keeping just to right of bend of By Brook. *Spire of Box church visible well ahead, above waters of stream.* Through squeeze stile in cross-hedge just to right of By Brook and keep beside this stream, with its rushes and ducks, passing a few gardens on slopes beyond. Over stile in fence and immediately turn right by small weir, with fence on right. Bear left, with part of now divided stream on left, onto well surfaced path. Over footbridge onto wood-chipping path and bear left over attractive arched footbridge. Now turn right with By Brook on immediate right and fence on left. Box Mill (now a theatre) over to left.

(E) Bear left with care onto road entering village of Box. Pass Box Mill on left and under busy railway line before taking **second** of two footpaths to right, initially down a surfaced roadway alongside house (Watch for this with care, as the **first** turn right heads for Bath on our Cross-Cotswold Pathway and also uses Macmillan Way Waymarks). At end of roadway go diagonally left across sports field keeping

Path beside the By Brook, approaching Saltbox Farm

off sensitive pitches and heading for point between cricket pavilion to left and tennis courts to right. Then bear left up roadway and turn right with great care, onto busy A4 using footpath on far side. *Situated above the valley of the By Brook, the substantial village of Box has a number of handsome stone houses, the great quarries here having supplied much of the stone used by the builders of its elegant, much larger neighbour, Bath. The long Box Tunnel was one of the great features of Brunel's Great Western railway line from London to Bristol and the south aisle of Box Church was specially built for the use of his great gang of navvies. Do not miss the Blind House, a quaint little village lockup to our left, along the north side of the A4.*

(F) Go a few yards along A4 and then turn left just before Jacob Baylay's Ale House on right, to go up narrow, stepped footpath between houses. Now cross A365 with care and go up narrow steps onto pathway between two walls (SP - *Public Footpath Henley*). At end of pathway turn left, then right crossing driveway to go over stile passing nursery on right. Go straight up field to gate with fence to immediate left, over another stile and go in same direction across meadow full of wild flowers. *Look back from here for fine views northwards up the valley of the By Brook.* Over stile beside metal gate and up another field keeping hedge and then wall on right, soon joining rough track. Pass converted barns on right. Over small stile and bear right onto road in hamlet of Henley. Turn left at road junction and follow road up out of Henley. Turn left by grassy triangle onto slightly busier road and into hamlet of Blue Vein. Pass houses on right and then turn right onto short track. Soon turn left onto busier road.

(G) Almost immediately turn right off road and through signed gap in wall. Head straight down edge of field keeping to immediate left of wall. Turn right through gap at end of field and then left to head down next field keeping to immediate right of hedge. Pass oak trees and soon turn right at end of field. *Now following course of Roman road that once ran from Silchester to Bath (not apparent)* and keep to immediate right of fence for short distance before turning left through special gap in fence. Now bear slightly left to go down to immediate left of hedge which continues alongside on right.

91

(A) At bottom, right-hand end of field, where four hedges meet, go diagonally right through gaps, across partly stone-lined ditch and up next field in same direction as previously, keeping to immediate right of hedge and soon ignoring gap to left. At top of rise bear left, still keeping to immediate right of hedge. Ignore another gap to left. Cross possibly boggy track in far corner of field and through large metal gate immediately ahead. Through this gate and bear left to follow up left-hand edge of field. Through large metal gate at top of field and turn left onto narrow road. Pass entrance drive to South Wraxall Manor on left (not signed) and smaller house on right (Mount Pleasant Farm).

(B) Soon turn right over stile (SP - *Public Path*). *(But first go a few yards further along road if you wish to have a brief glimpse of the lovely, partly-medieval manor house of South Wraxall through gates on left.)* Down right-hand edge of cricket field and over stile in corner. Turn right through possible squeeze-stile with house on immediate left and keep straight down driveway. Bear left onto better surfaced road into South Wraxall village with houses on both sides. Turn right at road junction by Willow Cottage and just beyond church, turn left onto wider road (SP - *Bradford-on-Avon*). Telephone box on right, opposite the Longs Arms. *There are several pleasant old stone houses close to the church, which has interesting features including a large squint and several handsome wall monuments.*

(C) Pass village hall on left and, opposite entrance to Church Fields housing estate, turn right through kissing gate. Follow path through kissing gate and go straight across field on surfaced path to Lower Wraxall. Through gate and bear left onto road opposite Mison's Farm. At end of wall, turn right through gate and along path with converted barns on right. Through kissing gate at end of small field and down path with wall on right and hedge on left. Straight, not left, and immediately cross stream onto narrow tarmac lane lined with pleasant old stone houses.

(D) Soon over x-rds onto narrow, but well surfaced road (signed-*No Through Road*). Pass Park Cottage on right. Ignore footpath sign on left, pass sign *Cherry Orchard Farm* on left, then pass Cherry Orchard farmhouse on right, where tarmac ends. Bend round to right on track which has hedges on both sides. Track now starts to ascend slightly where hedge on left changes to fence; ignore entrance to golf course on right, straight over dirt road with another entrance to golf course on right. Turn right at junction of tracks with bridleway coming in from left and pass Great Cumberwell Farm, largely to right. Keep on track as it bends to right by high stone wall on right and, ignoring large roadway to left, bear half-left onto moderately surfaced track with power-poles beside it. Pass edge of Cumberwell Park Golf Course on right and, after passing houses on both sides, cross the busy A363 with care at offset x-rds (SP - *Ashley*).

(E) Onto minor road (`7.5 tonnes restricted' sign) and, after 100 yards, turn left over stone stile. Cross field, half-right, aiming to

Town Bridge, Bradford-on-Avon

South Wraxall Manor

right-hand side of a line of oak trees and to right of large house with outstanding chimney, to a stone stile. Over stile and straight ahead to kissing gate beside field gate. Through kissing gate and go diagonally left, first aiming to right of line of ash trees and continue past kissing gate beyond trees on well-used path. *Spire of Christchurch, Bradford-on-Avon, visible ahead left.* Over stile and go diagonally left across recreation ground (fenced-off children's play-ground to left).

(F) Through gap in wall to right of metal gate and go slightly left to cross minor road (Ashley Road) at offset 'x-rds' at our entry to Bradford-on-Avon. Go down Huntingdon Street and then cross Winsley Road (B3108). Now go down steep, broad pathway of Conigre Hill. Bear left down steep lane passing Zion Baptist Chapel on right, then bear left ignoring sign *Middle Rank* to right. Turn right onto slightly busier road and almost immediately turn left down narrow pathway (opposite house numbered '62' and dated 1695). Turn sharp left and then turn right into Church Street by mill called Dutch Barton. *Plaque on wall states: 'Flemish weavers were brought to this area by clothiers Paul Methuen in 1659 and William Brewer in 1674. Improved techniques re-established the wool trade'.* Pass Abbey Mill on left and turn left over River Avon by footbridge *(but go straight ahead to visit the unique little Saxon church of St Lawrence, on right just beyond).* Good view to left of Abbey Mill *(flats)* when crossing footbridge and then turn left to follow short riverside path to south end of Town Bridge. *Ensure that time is spent looking round this beautiful old town, with its steep streets above the river enriched with many splendid examples of 17th- and 18th-century archi-tecture - evidence of its long enduring prosperity as a cloth manufacturing centre. In addition to the little Saxon church, see also the fine parish church opposite and the lovely old Town Bridge with its medieval arches and its stone capped 17th-century lock-up.*

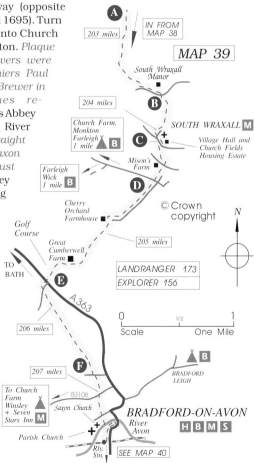

MAP 39

203 miles

IN FROM MAP 38

South Wraxall Manor

204 miles

Church Farm, Monkton Farleigh 1 mile

SOUTH WRAXALL

Village Hall and Church Fields Housing Estate

Mison's Farm

Farleigh Wick 1 mile

© Crown copyright

N

Cherry Orchard Farmhouse

Golf Course

Great Cumberwell Farm

205 miles

TO BATH

LANDRANGER 173
EXPLORER 156

A363

0   1/2   1
Scale   One Mile

206 miles

207 miles

BRADFORD LEIGH

To Church Farm Winsley + Seven Stars Inn

B3108

Saxon Church

Parish Church

BRADFORD-ON-AVON
River Avon

H B M S

Rly. Stn.

SEE MAP 40

93

Chapter 8 Bradford-on-Avon - Bruton 32 Miles

(A) Turn right at south end of Town Bridge to leave Bradford-on-Avon on St Margaret's Street (A363) and immediately pass Georgian Lodge Hotel on left. Straight over mini-roundabout leaving A363 and onto B3109 (SP - *Frome*) (road to railway station down to right). Pass attractive Hall's Charity Almshouses on left and over bridge crossing railway line. Keep straight on B3109, then turn right, off road between Canal Tavern and Lock Inn Cottage Tearooms, to go down Kennet and Avon Canal towpath. *This is part of the 84-mile-long Kennet and Avon Canal National Waterway Walk, which runs from Reading to Bath.* Pass short path to massive, 14th-century Bradford-on-Avon Tithe Barn on right - well worth a visit. Now on firm, wide towpath with woods up to left beyond tranquil waters of canal. Pass Barton Farm swing-bridge and foot-bridge on left, ignoring footpath waymark to left. Ruined mill on River Avon visible down to right near entry to Avoncliff hamlet. Turn right at aqueduct and then sharp left at Rennie House (B & B), Canal Bookshop and Cross Guns Inn, to go under this handsome 18th-century stone aqueduct - *one of a series constructed by John Rennie, the builder of the Kennet and Avon Canal.* Then bear left up steps onto surfaced road passing cafe and car park on right with Avonvilla (B&B) beyond, also on right.

(B) Go up road out of Avoncliff and soon, where road turns to left, go straight ahead through gap by large wooden gate and onto steep, winding path up through woods. Keep left at fork of tracks by stile down to right and soon bear left onto surfaced road at entry to Upper Westwood. Turn right at road junction by phone box and go straight, not left at next road junction by Chestnut Grove. Pass elegant, early-18th-century house on right and soon, after passing house *(Ashlers - No 130)* on right, turn left off road (probably SP - *Lower Westwood*) to go over stone stile and along narrow surfaced path between fences. Now go in same general direction on tarmac paths beside roads down through 'The Pastures' housing estate in Westwood. *Distant view ahead of the Westbury White Horse.*

(C) Bear right at end of estate onto busier road at end of Westwood. *(But turn left if you wish to visit National Trust's fine late 16th-century Westwood Manor - about half-a-mile.)* Bear left at road junction near coach entry to Iford Manor (no entry for walkers here) to go down Iford Hill. Go steeply down hill on road with wall of Iford Manor Gardens on right and soon also on left. Turn left over River Frome opposite Iford Manor on right, crossing bridge complete with figure of Britannia on its parapet. *Try to visit these delightful gardens - the creation of noted landscape architect, Sir Harold Peto, who lived here between 1899 and 1933.*

(D) At 150 yards beyond Iford Bridge, turn left over stile. Go across small field parallel with River Frome. Over stile to left of metal gate, still keeping parallel with river, soon passing attractive weir and into Somerset. Over stile beside metal gate  still keeping parallel with river. Farleigh Hungerford's thin church tower just visible on skyline ahead. Start to veer slightly right, away from course of river, following well-used track across field. Through kissing gate beside metal gate and aim across field towards church tower. Over stile beside metal gate and across field aiming for gate to right of Farleigh Hungerford castle ruins. Over stile beside metal gate and turn sharp left, keeping hedge on immediate left. In bottom corner of small field go over stile and sleeper bridge crossing small stream and bear left by trout farm on right, onto surfaced track. Impressive ruins of Farleigh Hungerford Castle above to right. Keep on track beyond battlements (do not go up steep and slippery slope to right).

Farleigh Hungerford Castle

(E) Turn sharp right onto busy A366 with great care and keep on this road, being ready to squeeze into verge when vehicles pass *(But turn right and go through gateway if you wish to visit 14th-century Farleigh Hungerford Castle, with its splendid chapel containing wall paintings, stained glass and the fine tomb of its builder, Sir Thomas Hungerford.)* Keep on A366 beyond castle but just before reaching Hungerford Arms, turn left onto minor road (SP - *Tellisford*) and pass Farleigh Hungerford church on right - *a pleasant little building with a thin tower and a mid-19th-century interior.* Soon pass small conical-roofed, stone water tower on left. Straight, not right at road junction at end of village and down hill overhung with horse-chestnut trees. Pass entrance on right to 19th-century neo-Gothic mansion, Farleigh Castle - now Farleigh College.

(F) At next valley bottom, over bridge crossing small stream and almost immediately turn left off road and over stile in hedge (difficult to spot in summer). Go straight across field to left of large ash tree and to right of terrace edge which descends to left. Through gate into woodlands and follow well-used path before emerging into more open field interspersed with trees. Cross field and go through gate. Turn right immediately beyond gate and walk up bank with wood on immediate right. At top of bank, go through hunting gate and follow field boundary with hedge on right, to corner with gateway. Turn left in this corner, passing gateway. Soon turn right through gate and on towards hornbeam hedge by Manor Farmhouse, keeping to immediate right of this hedge. Bear left at end of hedge, through gate and turn right onto farm drive. At end of farm drive bear right onto public road in Tellisford and, after about 50 yards, turn sharp left to go down pathway in front of handsome 18th-century Crabb House. Down steep cobbled path with handrail and cross mill stream by ruins of Tellisford Mill on right. Then cross River Frome by attractive arched bridge. Now back into Wiltshire for a short distance.

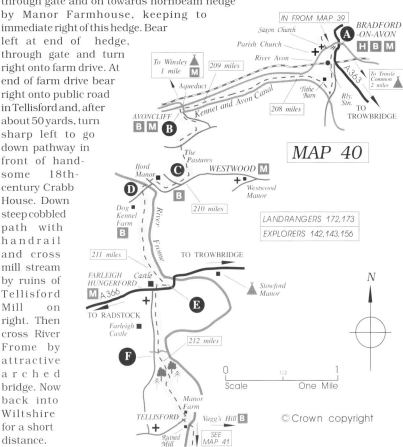

95

(A) Very soon turn right, leaving surfaced path and over metal stile. Go across field with River Frome some distance to right, soon passing weir on right. *World War II pillbox on right - probably part of a defensive line along the east bank of the Frome.* Over wooden stile beyond pillbox, with tranquil waters of River Frome also just to right. Keep to left-hand edge of field with wood on immediate left and then bear slightly to left to go through metal gate to left of small farm outbuildings onto surfaced road. Pass Langham Farmhouse on right - *delicious honey usually available here.* Along pleasant shady road with River Frome down to right. Pass anglers' car park on right, and now cross back into Somerset. Keep on track across more open field. Rode Church, with two unusual miniature 'spires' at its west end, soon visible ahead *(this is now a private dwelling)*. Over stile beside cattle-grid at entry to Rode and pass handsome 18th-century Langham Place on right.

(B) Cross busier road into High Street (SP - *Rode*) and soon bend round to right by small green with war memorial to left and pass bus shelter and phone box on left. Keep straight up High Street passing shop and old school building on left. Straight, not right, at end of village by Merfield Lodge and almost immediately turn left, up Crooked Lane. At T-junction at end of lane go straight ahead onto narrow trackway overhung with trees. Through gap in hedge and into field, now keeping in same direction with hedge-line on immediate left.

(C) Over stile at end of field and climb embankment to cross busy A36 with very great care. Go down embankment, then left along base of embankment, before going over stile on right and then keeping to left-hand edge of field. Over rudimentary stile into next field and keep on same line aiming for next stile. Over stile and go across recreation ground, veering right to avoid most of games pitches. Go through metal gate to left of club buildings, cross road *(but turn left if you wish to go to Little Chef and/or Travel Lodge)* and bear left at entry to village of Beckington, with its wealth of pleasant old stone buildings. Keep on road into Beckington and bear right in centre of village keeping on wider road (Frome Road) by Woolpack Inn on left (SP - *Oldford*). *But if you wish to explore, a little further on, just beyond the Woolpack Inn, a second road leads up left to the church with its outstandingly beautiful Norman tower and its interesting interior.*

(D) Pass bus stop on left and at far end of village, opposite layby on left, turn right up Stubbs Lane (track) by small conical roofed gazebo. Go down surfaced farm road for about 300 yards, then through small gate on left on to path encouraged by owner (SP - *Lullington*). Soon pass barn on right and continue between wire fence on left and on right, old hedge followed by Leylandii hedge. Where this ends, part of Orchardleigh Golf Course visible ahead across valley. Follow path as it turns sharp right down steep hill with steps at bottom. Continue on path to clearly visible footbridge. *World War II pillbox over to right, on banks of River Frome - similar to the one just beyond Tellisford.* Creamery chimney visible up valley to left.

(E) Over stile and wooden footbridge across River Frome and go diagonally right to cross stile at right-hand corner of narrow field. Cross road and over stile. Up small bank and turn right to follow to immediate left of trees and hedge lining small tributary stream, with

Tellisford Bridge (see page 95)

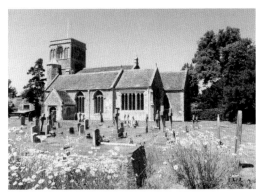

Beckington Church

edge of Orchardleigh Golf Course to left. Cross surfaced drive with bridge to immediate right, with views up drive beyond to attractive early 19th-century 'Gothick' gate-house, known as Gloucester Lodge. Pass waymark on post and after 50 yards turn right onto track at second waymark, also on post. Through small wooden gate beside large one and bear left onto surfaced road with cottage down to right. Bear left onto road near phone box at entry to village of Lullington and almost immediately left by attractive green complete with old hand-pump. *The church is over to the right, beyond the green, and is one of the more interesting ones to be found on our route. See especially the north doorway, the font and the tower arches - all beautiful specimens of Norman craftsmanship.* Pass Yew Tree House on left and Gloucester Farm on left.

(F) Where road bends sharply right, go straight ahead through gate, keeping hedge on left. Follow farm track to go through gate and continue across field to right of wooded hedge. Bear very slightly left to stile in wire fence. Over stile and, with eyes open for possibly hazardous golf balls, keep more or less in same direction across golf course in Orchardleigh Park, heading towards right-hand end of old stable building passing between two pond hazards. Victorian Orchardleigh House now visible over to left. Arrive at post on surfaced road with a number of waymarks and bear half right onto this road. Ignore sign on left to church. After 500 yards go through modest gate and cattle-grid at exit from Golf Club.

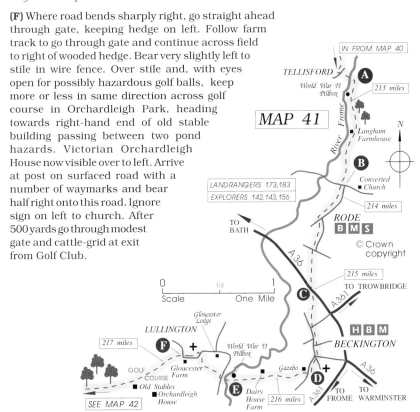

IN FROM MAP 40

TELLISFORD

World War II Pillbox

A · 213 miles

MAP 41

River Frome

N

■ Langham Farmhouse

B

Converted ■ Church

214 miles

LANDRANGERS 173,183
EXPLORERS 142,143,156

TO BATH

RODE
B **M** **S**

© Crown copyright

215 miles
TO TROWBRIDGE

A36

A361

C

Scale   0   1/2   1   One Mile

Gloucester Lodge

LULLINGTON

217 miles   **F** ✚

World War II Pillbox

GOLF COURSE   Gloucester Farm
■ Old Stables
■ Orchardleigh House

SEE MAP 42

Gazebo ■ ✚

E Dairy House Farm   216 miles   **D**

H **B** **M**

BECKINGTON

A36

A361

TO FROME   TO WARMINSTER

97

(A) *(Take great care to keep on right course from here onwards - we route planners lost ourselves here - twice!)* Beyond gate at end of Orchardleigh Golf Club, bear half-right, off roadway, and (going almost due west) keep along left-hand edge of large pheasant pen to join track in same direction at beginning of woodland near waymark. After 150 yards cross another track with several buildings and pens to left, continuing in same direction. After 250 yards main track turns sharp right, but keep on grassy path due west for 100 yards.

(B) Leave wood through gap to right of broken stile and over small sleeper bridge into field with woodlands still on right-hand side. Head straight down ever-narrowing field, initially with wood on right and then only hedge with trees. Go through gateway, bear slightly left and immediately through gap beyond, at meeting of four fields, ignoring grassy track up to left. Follow track at edge of field with hedge and stream on right, at first a little north of west, then sharp left, continue to follow hedge as it turns right and stream and cross wooden footbridge. Go diagonally up large, steeply sloping field aiming for clump of pine trees. Over stile to left of metal gate at top of field, at entry to attractive stone and thatch, hill-top village of Buckland Dinham and go beside wall, up short lane leading to church.

(C) Pass lych gate on right, *noting church with its Norman south doorway within a splendidly vaulted porch and its fine Perpendicular tower, and also the little village lockup opposite the church.* Turn left down small road from church passing phone box on right and turn right onto busy A362 opposite village hall. After about 100 yards, turn left just beyond bus shelter on right, go up small tarmac lane between houses *(but go straight for Bell Inn).* Go onto narrow path, first tarmac and then grassy, to go through kissing gate and over stile. Now bear slightly left in narrow field keeping wall and then hedge on immediate left. Distant view ahead of Alfred's Tower (see pages 102-103), on wooded northerly confines of Stourhead Estate. Over stone stile and go down field keeping hedge on immediate left. Over stile to left, down across field to go over stile and then cross minor road.

(D) Immediately over stone stile beyond road. Continue in same direction across field aiming for stile at end of field. Over stile, sleeper bridge and second stile and veer diagonally half-right (almost due south) aiming to left of two ash trees on right-hand edge of large field. Through gate, over track and bear right through gap to follow slight incline up right-hand edge of narrow field. Over stile in hedge beneath small oak tree and turn left to go down minor road. Go along road for about 500 yards, then under railway bridge and go another 500 yards before bearing right onto busier road at entry to quiet village of Great Elm, poised above wooded valley of Mells Stream.

(E) After 200 yards, where road bends round to right, bear left by metal bollard, and down steep little tree-shaded path with walls on either side *(but go straight ahead if you wish to visit early Norman church - on right after 150 yards).* At bottom of path turn sharp left onto minor road, then bear right over bridge crossing Mells Stream, here dammed up to form attractive duckpond. Ignore footpath signs to right *(unless you wish to divert to Mells - fine church and hospitable Talbot Inn - under two miles)* and keep on road as it bends left up through woodland. Halfway up hill turn right onto track in wood *joining the East Mendip Way - a 19-mile County Path between Frome and Wells.* Bear right at top of track and follow well-used path within wood with its fenced edge close

Duckpond at Great Elm

to left. Happily there is little sign of the great quarries ahead right *(loud blasting sometimes takes place)*, but railway line and Mells Stream are just visible down to right in places. Path starts to ascend a little before going between two massive stones at Murder Combe *(we could find no clues as to the origin of this place-name)*.

(F) Turn left with care onto busy road and almost immediately turn right to go over stile onto track. Along track bending slightly to right, with hedge on immediate left, trees to right, the latter soon finishing as track peters out. Through pasture field still keeping hedge and then fence on left. Whatley church spire eventually visible ahead. *Now leaving the course of the East Mendip Way which turns right.* Go over stile in hedge keeping on same line along right-hand edge of next field with hazel hedge on immediate right. Over stile to left of water trough and keep along next field with hedge on immediate right, still aiming for Whatley church spire. Turn right, over stile in corner of field and turn immediately left to go over stile in cross hedge a few yards out from left. Now veer left to cross small portion of field diagonally and over stile in left-hand hedge. Up narrow path into fragmented village of Whatley with hedge on left and fence on right and pass bungalow called *Fortywinks* on right. Down tarmac driveway for a few yards before bearing left onto parallel path. Soon re-join driveway, bearing right where track comes in from left.

(G) Now bear left with care onto minor road by entry to Whatley Vineyard. Walk along road with care for about 100 yards and turn right onto track to immediate right of Sun Inn. Soon over stile into field and follow waymark arrow, bearing slightly left and aiming well to right of Alfred's Tower on skyline and water trough in middle of field, to go across field aiming (approximately) south-westwards) for kissing gate when it becomes visible. Through kissing gate, leaving right-of-way and turn left (south-east) onto permissive path to right of hedge *(kindly allowed by Mr John Norris)*. Climb railed fence and cross road to go down good track *(also permissive, and kindly allowed by Mr Christopher White)*.

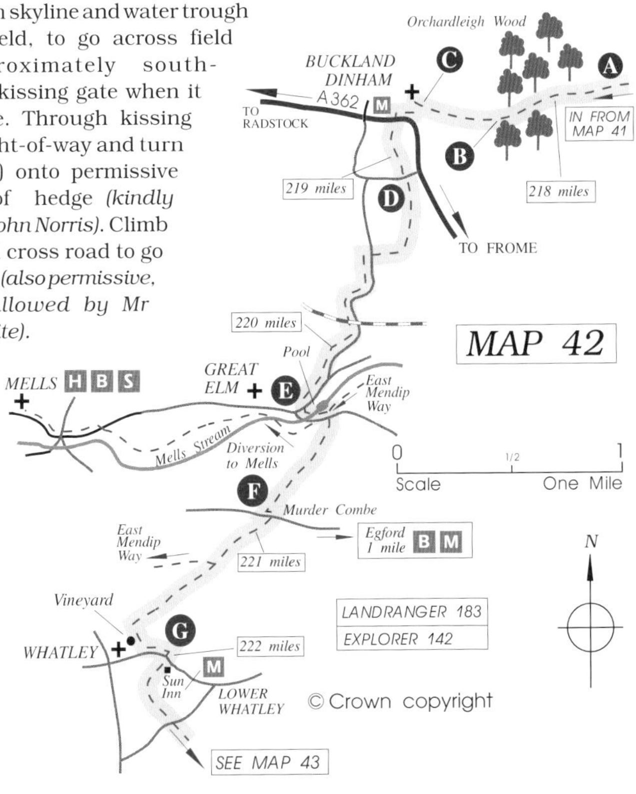

MAP 42

© Crown copyright

(A) After about 150 yards cross Nunney Brook in Nunney Combe re-joining right-of-way and immediately turn right onto path with Nunney Brook now on right. Pass small plantation of poplars on right. Pass sewage works over to right and horse jumps in field. Keep straight across rough field (ignoring bridge and kissing gate to right). Through kissing gate after meadow narrows considerably and into park-like garden of Combe Farm, farmhouse visible up to right beyond stream. Walk up tree-lined drive and through gate. Onto road, passing house with high wall on right and drop down into delightful village of Nunney.

(B) Turn right onto Frome Road by Rose Cottage and go through village, with restored market cross, duckpond and castle on right and church on left. *With its moat and elegant round towers, Nunney has a real flavour of France - everyone's dream of a perfect medieval castle. Its builder, Sir John de la Mare, lies in the church opposite, which also has fine monuments in its north aisle chapel and a Norman font with a Jacobean conical font cover.* Pass 'The George at Nunney' Hotel on left and Market Place with village shop on right. Go straight, not right by phone box (SP - *Witham Friary*). Head up hill out of village and fork left by Nunney First School walking with care on busier road.

(C) In Nunney Catch hamlet go straight ahead to immediate left of Theobald Arms, leaving road and down cul-de-sac to go under subway beneath very busy A361 *(but bear right keeping on road by Theobald Arms for Little Chef, by roundabout a short distance ahead)*. Beyond subway bear left onto still busy minor road. Walk down road **with great care** going straight, not left near Pyle Farm, where entry to Trudoxhill is signed. Pass chapel on left and keep straight through Trudoxhill until forking left (SP - *Marston*) by White Hart Inn. Leave village on road ignoring footpath signs to left.

(D) Where road bends sharply to left (about 200 yards beyond village) go straight ahead through metal gate and continue in same direction, across right-hand side of field, aiming for Nutty Coppice Farmhouse. Through metal gate in cross-hedge and over next field aiming for stile in line with farmhouse. Over stile in cross-hedge and, veering slightly right, aim for right-hand end of farm buildings. Over stile in coner of field and along path with farm buildings over to left. Soon over stile, up short farm drive to join road and fork left (SP - *Gare Hill*).

(E) Almost immediately turn right off road and through bushes to go to right of main bus garage at back of Lawns Farm. Over stile below large oak tree and go down long, narrow field with oak trees on both sides. Turn left through gateway in far left-hand

corner of field and bear left to corner of next field. Alfred's Tower (see pages 102-103) now visible at southern end of long, wooded ridge ahead. Soon aim for large metal gate to left of water trough. Through this gate and keep down field with hedge to immediate left, passing under pylon line. Through wooden gate and down fenced farm track. Through metal gate and turn left onto road and soon over Witham Bridge crossing infant River Frome. *(Note attractive fishing lakes back right. These were once used by the monks of Witham Priory - see below.)* Turn right, leaving road opposite large concrete silage store of Witham Hall Farm, and over stile by large metal gate. Up field keeping to immediate right of hedge.

The fields to left were once covered by buildings of a large Carthusian Priory, known latterly as Witham Friary. The

Nunney Castle

remaining earthworks are not very revealing but a large priory was established here as part of Henry II's penance for the murder of Archbishop Thomas Becket in 1170. This was the first and mother house of the Carthusians in England, the Carthusians being the strictest and most austere of all religious orders. It was dissolved in 1539 and its buildings were acquired by Ralph Hopton, who converted them into a residence. This was purchased by Sir William Wyndham in the 18th century and he built a fine Palladian mansion here, Witham House, to the design of William Talman. The house then passed into the hands of Alderman Beckford who started to build a new house on a small hill nearby, but he died long before it was completed and the energies of his eccentric son, the noted William Beckford, were soon concentrated on the building of the equally ill-fated Fonthill. Thus the mansion at Witham fell into disrepair and now nothing remains apart from the long, straight green roads which we shall use shortly - they were once part of the grandiose approach drive to the mansion.

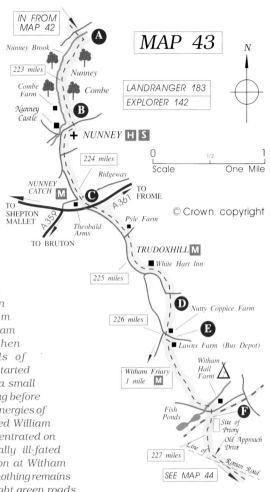

(F) Over stile and cross very busy railway line with great care - 'Stop, Look, Listen' as the notice states. The trains may not go as fast as their French or Japanese counterparts, but they are still extremely dangerous. Over second stile and up field in same direction, keeping to immediate right of hedge. Gare Hill Church visible in gap in trees on ridge ahead left. Through metal gate and go across field veering only slightly left of previous line and once over brow, aim for stile in hedge. Over stile adjacent to hunting rails and go down long, wide green-road with hedges on both sides *(this was part of the old approach drive to long-vanished Witham House - see above).* Just before reaching Walk Farm, cross course of Roman road that once ran from Salisbury to the lead mines near Charterhouse in the Mendips, although there are no obvious signs here.

(A) Through metal gate and pass to immediate left of Walk Farm. Initially keep in same direction, crossing two farm tracks by farmhouse on right. Through metal gate and bear right beyond last buildings over to right, keeping on wide farm track between hedges - a continuation of green-road. Now heading straight towards wooded ridge marking border with Wiltshire. Through metal gate at end of track, but green-road still continues with hedges on both sides.

(B) The surfaced farm track continues in a straight line with hedge and Pound Copse on right, going through four more metal gates and starting to climb gently. Splendid views opening up behind (northwards). Pass farm buildings on right, through metal gate and pass drive to Witham Park Farm's farmhouse on right.

(C) At entry to Witham Park woodlands, turn right onto permissive forest track. After about two-thirds of a mile cross over open space where forest tracks join, keeping in same direction for half a mile to come to wooden gate. Turn right onto road and where it bends to right, go straight ahead into West End Wood, through wooden gate onto permissive forest track, ignoring track up hill to left with *No Through Road* sign. Continue on track passing brick building in trees on right and bear left up slight rise with good views to right where trees are thin. Bear right and track becomes worn and boggy in parts.

(D) Over stile, turn right onto road and shortly after passing Druly Hill Farm on right, turn left off road at entry to Forestry Commission's King's Wood Warren woodlands, by going through small gate. Go down well surfaced forest road, very soon ignoring small pathway up to left. Keep straight at Y-junction, going upwards (rather than right, downwards). Pleasant track at start with woods to right and bracken covered slopes up to left with trees beyond (but character of woods will change many times before we arrive in vicinity of Alfred's Tower - still some way ahead). Keep on track where it bends to right, thus going onto a short permissive section and ignoring path up to left. Woodlands now on both sides. At next junction of tracks, keep straight, going upwards, not right. Pass large wooden foresters' hut on left. Fork left off main track to join narrower track (Notice on right of main track states *No unauthorised vehicles*). Continue along track and ignore small stile on right with waymark. Forest ends on right, with field beyond line of beech trees on right of path. Go onto public road.

(E) Go straight over this road with care, joining the Leland Trail (see below) (SP - *Aaron's Hill*). *But turn left and go up wooded hill on road for 250 yards if you wish to visit the National Trust's Alfred's Tower, on right of road at top of hill. This massive 160ft-high, triangular tower in mellow brick was built in 1772 to mark the place where King Alfred probably set up his standard in the year 878 at the start of his eventually successful campaign to repel the Danes. It contains a staircase and can be climbed when open.*

Alfred's Tower also marks the start of the Leland Trail, a 28-mile walking route ending at Ham Hill, near Montacute. This was developed by South Somerset District Council and we shall follow it for about 17 miles, only leaving it at South Cadbury. It is named after the 16th-century antiquary, John Leland, who travelled through Somerset at some time between 1535 and 1543 while compiling his great 'Itinerary'.

Alfred's Tower

It is also possible to walk beyond Alfred's Tower down to the National Trust's elegant Palladian mansion of Stourhead and its magnificently landscaped gardens - a distance of just over two miles. The path drops down through pleasant woodlands, joining a minor road into Stourton village by Stourhead's Rock Arch.

(E) If you have diverted from main route, now return to beginning of footpath at bottom of hill (SP - *Penselwood*) and turning left into more woods. Go straight, not left at Y-junction of paths. Go straight, not right, at next Y-junction of paths and start to drop into valley. Bear left joining footpath with waymarks pointing both ways and almost immediately bear left again at T-junction of tracks. Now climb up track as it bends to right and, at top of slope, keep straight where another track comes in from left.

(F) Turn right at cross-roads of tracks and then bear right onto surfaced road. Pass through security barrier and follow road as it bends to left and right. Then where road bends again to left, fork right up track (SP - *Redlynch 3 miles*). Go uphill through barrier on sunken trackway in Black-slough Wood and then start to descend slightly. Fork right at junction of tracks and footpaths and continue down hill. Straight, not right, keeping on main track soon passing rhododendrons on right before forking left. Over stile beside metal gate and pass field to right, with woods still to left. Continue in same direction on track across field as woods end on left, and soon go straight, not right, to pass along left-hand side of small wood.

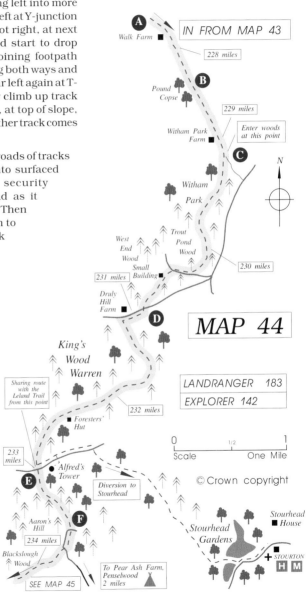

IN FROM MAP 43

Walk Farm

228 miles

Pound Copse

229 miles

Witham Park Farm

Enter woods at this point

N

Witham Park

Trout Pond Wood

West End Wood

230 miles

Small Building

231 miles

Druly Hill Farm

MAP 44

King's Wood Warren

LANDRANGER 183

EXPLORER 142

Sharing route with the Leland Trail from this point

232 miles

■ *Foresters' Hut*

0   1/2   1
Scale   One Mile

© Crown copyright

233 miles

Alfred's Tower

Diversion to Stourhead

Stourhead House

Aaron's Hill

Stourhead Gardens

234 miles

Blackslough Wood

STOURTON

SEE MAP 45

To Pear Ash Farm, Penselwood 2 miles

(A) At far corner of wood, bear half-right across field aiming for stile. Over pair of stiles and cross next field. *From here we shall go in an almost straight line for over two miles, following the course of a supposed 'old coach road' until reaching Redlynch. However, this was probably a drive to the mansion of Redlynch, connecting it with the coach road from London and also perhaps with Stourhead. Sometimes known as the Hard Way, it may also have been used by drovers taking cattle to the London markets.* Pass wood on immediate right (this is the remains of Stavordale Wood which appears to have been largely cleared on the left (south) side). Path soon becomes a track again. Over stile beside gate; wood still on right, hedge on left. Through metal gate and continue on fenced track. Good views of Alfred's Tower back right. At T-junction of tracks go straight across and over stile on other side. Cross field in same direction and through wooden gate. Go straight up field and through wooden gate. Keep in same direction on farm track and through wooden gate. Keep straight through Coachroad Farm's farmyard, with barn to left and farmhouse to right.

(B) Over stile at end of yard, cross road and over second stile (SP - *Redlynch*). Keep in same direction across field, over stile beside metal gate and across small field on track. Good views northwards over low rolling country and back, eastwards, to Alfred's Tower. Over stile beside metal gate and continue on track across next field. Foundations of `Old Coach Road' visible in grass here. Pass small wood known as Walk Copse on left, over stile beside metal gate and continue straight across next field following slightly raised course of old road. Over stile beside metal gate and pass substantial farm with large garden and pool beyond fence to right.

(C) Follow to immediate left of wire fence and up slight incline across large field. At end of large field, over stile just beyond thatched Moor Wood Cottage on left. Go between wire fences, follow round to left of small outbuilding and head diagonally left to go over stile beside wooden gate. Resume original line of walk by going up track with fence to right and attractive open woodlands known as Moor Wood to left. Over stile beside metal gate at end of wood on left. Continue across field up avenue of young oaks.

Packhorse Bridge at Bruton

(D) Over pair of stiles and turn right with care onto busy B3081 opposite gateway to Redlynch Park - our first significant change of direction for over two miles. *Redlynch, much altered following a disastrous fire, was the home of that great 18th-century politician, Charles James Fox.* Keep well into side of road and soon turn left at cross-roads (SP - *Shepton Montague*). Pass Redlynch Farm on right and beyond houses on right turn right, off road, opposite handsome little 18th-century Redlynch Church and over stile beside metal gate (SP - *Bruton*). Head up right-hand side of field with hedge on immediate right and over pair of stiles and sleeper bridge in top right-hand corner of field. Initially keep to immediate left of hedge, but when this turns right, go straight across field keeping just to right of small mound and soon aiming for stile. Over stile beside metal gate, keep down field in same direction with hedge to immediate right. *Glastonbury Tor visible well over to left.*

(E) Pass hedge with Droppinglane Farm's buildings beyond to right and over stile to right of bushes. Bear left, maintaining same line as previously, to go over stile beside metal gate. Now veer slightly left to go across field keeping just to left of hedge-line. Over stile about three yards to right of metal gate, keep down field to immediate left of hedge. Almost at bottom of field, turn right through hedge on right, crossing pair of stiles and sleeper bridge. Go down field keeping to right of hedge and after 150 yards, where hedge veers to left, go diagonally across field to stile at bottom of field. Bruton Dovecot visible well ahead left.

(F) Over this stile beside metal gate, turn right onto minor road and immediately turn left with care onto B3081 (not signed). After about 40 yards fork left off B3081 onto minor road *(7.5 tonne* Restriction Sign*)*. Take care on narrow, but quite busy road with virtually no verges. *Pass field entry to National Trust's impressive 16th-century dovecot, above to right. This once belonged to Bruton Abbey.* At entry to Bruton, turn right into Godminster Lane, over bridge crossing railway line and bear right onto wider road (Silver Street) (no sign). Go along Silver Street passing buildings of King's School on both sides, including precinct wall of Bruton's once great abbey on right. At this point the intrepid can cross the little River Brue by turning left and using stepping stones, although the more cautious walker will turn left just beyond to go over attractive packhorse bridge.

But go straight ahead if first wishing to visit church - on right just beyond. This is a splendid, largely Perpendicular style building, with an early 14th-century crypt, a tall graceful tower, and an unusually elegant Roccoco chancel. The latter comes as a shock when a medieval interior is expected, but it is very impressive. See also the fine early Renaissance tomb in a recess in the chancel, with the reclining figure of Sir Maurice Berkeley, who died in 1506 and who was Standard Bearer to Henry VII, Henry VIII, Edward VI and Queen Elizabeth). Bruton is a delightful little town, as yet unspoilt by tourism. Its narrow High Street is lined with small shops and inns and, near its western end, the attractive Sexey's Hospital - almshouses complete with chapel and hall. Douglas Macmillan, the founder of the organisation now known as Macmillan Cancer Relief, went to Sexey's School, the buildings of which lie to the south-west of the town. For more details about Douglas Macmillan, see page 8.

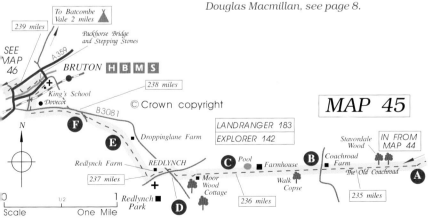

Chapter 9   Bruton - Abbotsbury   51 Miles

(A) To resume our walk - turn left beyond Bruton's packhorse bridge (or nearby stepping stones) into Lower Backway. Go straight along Lower Backway *(but turn right up one of several narrow passages (known locally as 'bartons') if you wish to visit shops or inns in the High Street)*. Turn right at end of Lower Backway and soon turn left by Town Mill House into far end of High Street to pass phone box on left.

(B) At end of High Street, go straight over road with care at Y-junction and, beside right-hand end of garage, up narrow Trendle Lane. Where tarmac driveway bends to left, go straight on up sunken trackway overhung with trees. By farm gates on right, follow track as it veers slightly right and becomes wider farm track. At about highest point, hedge to left ends, but track continues with hedge on right.

(C) Turn right to cross stile and go immediately left to follow close to right of hedge. *Good view ahead right includes Glastonbury Tor and, on a clear day, the distant line of the Quantocks.* Where this short hedge turns to left, veer half-right to go over field to stile in cross-fence. Keep in same direction down bank aiming for stile. Over offset pair of stiles crossing concrete farm road *(which, temptingly, leads down left to road on our route beyond Wyke Champflower - see Map - but is not a right-of-way!)* and go straight across field aiming well to right of buildings, one of which is on a mound. *These buildings include mellow-stoned Wyke Champflower Manor, to which is attached a small but most interesting church. Built in the 17th century, it has a delightfully unspoilt interior complete with elaborate stone pulpit, a painted tympanum dividing the ceilings of the chancel and nave and also Jacobean box pews, each with its own hat peg.*

(D) Turn left onto road, soon passing driveway to Wyke Champflower's manor and church on left *(do try to visit this)* and then over bridge crossing remains of railway (the old Somerset and Dorset line). Immediately turn left at road junction keeping on road. Under railway bridge just beyond modern house on left and continue along road, ignoring waymark up to left where our road bends sharply down to right. Down this narrow sunken road to go under yet another railway bridge.

(E) Over bridge crossing the River Brue and turn right at T-junction in Cole hamlet by Manor House on right. *Douglas Macmillan must have walked through this hamlet many hundreds of times on his daily journey between his home at Castle Cary and his school at Bruton - almost three miles each way.* Keep on road passing Manor Farm and Cole Farmhouse, both on right. Where road bears left beyond Cole Farm, fork right and over stile (SP - *Ridge Hill*). Go diagonally left, down to far corner of field, then bear right into corner, go over stile and cross brook on concrete bridge. Go up through orchard to waymark, turn left and walk along upper edge of orchard with hedge on right. Over stile at top corner of orchard and up field with hedge to immediate right. Pleasant views across orchards in valley to left. *Alfred's Tower still visible beyond Bruton, with the latter's church tower and dovecote well in view.* At

top of Ridge Hill bear left following fence line to immediate right. Bear right still following fence line to right, with small valley coming up from left. Turn right going over stile in far right-hand corner and across small field with hedge on left.

(F) Over stile, down sunken path and turn left onto sunken roadway. Ignore bridleway sign to left, and soon turn right (SP - *Ansford*) up sunken trackway, known as Solomon's Lane. This narrows in part to become pathway pleasantly overhung with bushes. Track starts to drop by stout wooden fence on right and outskirts of Higher Ansford just visible ahead. Straight, not right, at junction of sunken tracks and then turn right onto road in Higher Ansford by Ansford Farmhouse. Soon turn left at road junction by elegantly porched 18th-century Ansford House and down Ansford Road into Castle Cary. Pass turning to car park on right and turn right at T-junction by Highfield House into Castle Cary's High Street. *(But turn left and go up street for about 100 yards to look at house where Douglas Macmillan spent his early years - marked with a plaque.)* This is the start of **Macmillan Way West**, our branch route which heads across the Somerset Levels, the Quantocks and Exmoor to Barnstaple - a total distance of 102 miles.

Castle Cary is a delightful little market town situated below the earthworks of its early 12th-century castle, with colourful shops, hotels and inns - all full of character. The Victorian Market Hall is now partly a museum and Tourist Information Centre. Just behind it is the handsome 18th-century stone Post Office and the Round House or Pepper Pot, a stout little circular lock-up built in 1779. Douglas Macmillan was born in Castle Cary in 1884 and grew up here (see also page 8).

(G) Pass Market Hall on right and turn left immediately beyond George Hotel and go up Paddock Drain, a narrow, ascending passage (note vine on wall of George Hotel to left). Through kissing gate near Castle Cary Castle explanatory board and turn left following left-hand of two waymarks. Go straight up hill with fence line to immediate left. *Soon pass earthworks of castle to immediate right but these are better viewed from above, a few minutes walk along path. Glastonbury Tor soon visible, back over the town.* Through kissing gate in cross-fence and continue in same line before bearing right to aim for interesting observation point and benches near top of Lodge Hill. *With topograph and telescope, this makes a fine viewing (and resting!) point, with Mendips, Glastonbury Tor, Somerset Levels and Quantocks - all visible on a clear day.* Continue in same direction, with hedge over to left and go through kissing gate beside metal gate. Keep in same direction and then, just beyond concrete water trough, ignore stile ahead and turn left through kissing gate in fence. Now head southwards with fence to immediate right, soon passing storage tank and low farm building on right.

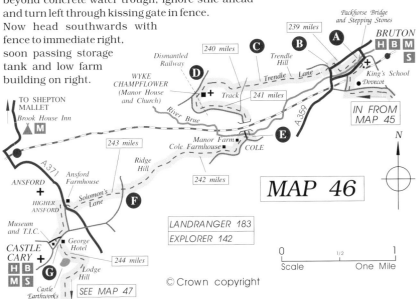

© Crown copyright

107

(A) Cross farm track, through kissing gate beyond it and initially go along field with fence to right. Soon turn right through kissing gate just beyond metal gate and veer to right of previous line to go to right-hand end of projecting cross-wall with hedge. Once round this corner follow down field to immediate right of field edge. Just before cross-fence ahead turn left through kissing gate and go up left-hand edge of field. Bear right at end of field to go through gate in front of electricity sub-station and turn left onto A359. Walk down A359 with great care and soon, first ignoring tempting track down to right, turn right through hunting gate just beyond it (SP - Hick's Lane, Yarlington). Down field with large hedge and overgrown trackway to immediate right and through metal gate. Keep down next field with hedge on right.

(B) Through hunting gate at end of field, joining track known as Hick's Lane, keeping in same direction. Lane eventually becomes sunken with overhanging trees and banks perforated by fox earths. At end of lane go straight ahead onto road.

(C) After 200 yards turn right over stile beside large metal gates (SP - Brookhampton). Straight across field, first going just to left of concrete water trough and then past oak and ash tree to stile well beyond. Over stile in cross-hedge and go diagonally left across slightly smaller field to far left-hand corner, keeping just to left of another single oak tree. Small stream now over to left - this is River Cam, which flows into River Yeo just to east of Yeovilton. Over sleeper bridge crossing smaller stream and over stile just beyond. Over even smaller field heading for corner in bushes, with stream still to immediate left. Over double-stile and across small orchard still keeping stream to immediate left. Over double-stile with sleeper bridge between and across next field with stream and hedge to left. Just before corner of field, turn left to cross stile and concrete and steel bridge over stream. Immediately turn right with River Cam and line of alder trees now on right. At end of field, turn right before reaching house and go back over River Cam on stone bridge.

(D) Cross small lawn and over stile in wall to left of drive gates, to turn left onto road, known here as Sandbrook Lane. Pass millhouse with re-located water wheel

and extensive garden on left. Go straight, not left, at road junction by Bridge Cottage on left. After about 300 yards fork left over stile off Sandbrook Lane (SP - Brookhampton). Now continue in same direction along narrow field, keeping parallel with roadside hedge to right and stream to left. Turn left over stile by metal gate re-joining Sandbrook Lane and cross bridge over River Cam.

(E) Soon, after road bends to right, turn left, up steps and over stile. Go diagonally across field and over stile in far left-hand corner. Along field keeping hedge on immediate left, over stile and continue along left-hand edge of North Cadbury School playing-field. Over stile and keep straight along path with hedges on both sides. Fork right (ignoring SP - Woolston) *(Now leaving originally planned Leland Trail, although, like us, many walkers now follow road to avoid dangerous crossing of A303)*. Over bridge and along often muddy path. Soon onto surfaced driveway and bear left onto road (Cutty Lane) at entry to quiet

The Catash Inn, North Cadbury

village of North Cadbury. Turn right at end of Cutty Lane into High Street and then turn left just beyond Catash Inn. Pass bus shelter and phone box on right.

(F) Straight, not left at end of village, keeping on road (SP - *South Cadbury*) *(but turn left for small Post Office stores)*. After about 100 yards, pass steps on left up to path leading to North Cadbury Church. *This fine church stands beside the equally impressive Elizabethan mansion of North Cadbury Court, and is well worth a short diversion. Its beautiful chancel was built to accommodate a college of priests, although for some reason this institution was never established. Beneath the tower is a handsome monument to Lady Botreaux, the builder of most of the church and to her husband, William. The magnificent roof is supported on angel corbel figures and light floods in through much clear glass - always a welcome change after the dark Victorian stained glass encountered in so many churches. There are also old flagged floors, a number of 16th-century carved bench ends and, in the vestry, a medieval alphabet for the instruction of children.* Now head southwards down road with great care. *Good views of wooded slopes of Cadbury Castle (hill fort) ahead.* Pass Chapel Cross Cottage on left and straight, not right by small thatched chapel attached to cottage, over to right. *This was noted by Tudor antiquary, John Leland who wrote, 'I turnid flat west by a little chapelle'.*

(G) However, our own route continues southwards (SP-*South Cadbury*), going over bridge crossing busy A303 and then straight, not right (SP - *South Cadbury*). Keep on road into South Cadbury, *a small village dominated by the impressive earthworks of Cadbury Castle, which rises just beyond.* Keep straight through South Cadbury, passing phone box on right. Go over x-rds by Red Lion Inn (SP - *Corton Denham*), finally leaving the Leland Trail. Pass church on right. *This has a late-14th-century tower but almost all of the rest was rebuilt in Victorian times.*

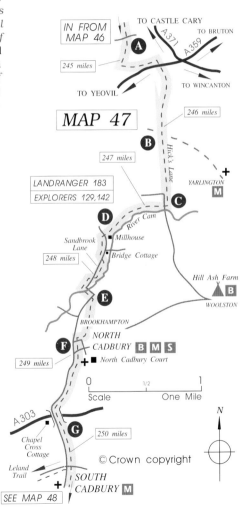

IN FROM MAP 46

TO CASTLE CARY

TO BRUTON

A371   A359

A

245 miles

TO YEOVIL

TO WINCANTON

246 miles

MAP 47

B

247 miles

Hick's Lane

YARLINGTON
M

LANDRANGER 183
EXPLORERS 129,142

C

D

River Cam

Sandbrook Lane   ■ Millhouse

248 miles   ■ Bridge Cottage

Hill Ash Farm
▲ **B**

WOOLSTON

E

BROOKHAMPTON

NORTH
CADBURY **B M S**

F

249 miles   ■ North Cadbury Court

0   1/2   1
Scale   One Mile

N

A303

G   250 miles

Chapel
Cross
Cottage

Leland
Trail

SOUTH
CADBURY **M**

© Crown copyright

SEE MAP 48

(A) Soon go straight, not right, keeping on road. *But turn right if you wish to climb up steep track to Cadbury Castle earthworks, from which there are outstanding views - a strongly recommended diversion - even for the weariest of walkers!). Cadbury Castle is a massive, 18-acre Iron Age hill fort at the meeting point of a number of ancient trackways. It is guarded by four massive banks and ditches and is likely to have been a key fortress during the years following the withdrawal of the Roman legions - the Celtic twilight. Referring to this fort, our friend the antiquary, John Leland states that, 'The people can telle nothing ther but that they have hard say that Arture much resorted to Camalat', and this place may at least have partly inspired the legends of Arthur and his Knights of the Round Table. However, extensive excavations in the 1960s sadly failed to solve this, its greatest mystery. So, having sampled the outstanding views from its ramparts, let us cease to dream ---* and instead, drop down to the road and head southwards once again soon passing small car park on left. Straight, not left, at road junction well beyond village keeping on Church Road and then turn left at next road junction (SP - *Corton Denham*).

(B) At T-junction below hill go almost straight across, onto path ahead between hedges (SP - *Stafford's Green*) and soon through gate. Bear right and up around hill slope along a narrow grassy hollow. Good views backwards from top of rise, to Cadbury Castle earthworks with their grassy summit and wooded fringe. Bear left through gate into next field and follow line of fence and hawthorn trees on left. Sutton Montis, *'the village south of the mount'*, visible to right. We shall now follow crest of Corton Ridge for over a mile. Go through stile beside gate into next field with fine views to right, across broad Yeo valley and later also to left, over low stone wall towards green rounded hills - the Beacon and Corton Hill, with village of Corton Denham, nestling between the two ridges. Keep field boundary to left, go through gate into next field and keep alongside wire fence and scrubby trees.

(C) Bear left through field gates into Ridge Lane, but continue southwards by immediately turning right into field keeping hedge on left. Through three gates into next fields, still keeping hedge on left. (At third gate, route now runs just inside county of Dorset - note Dorset CC waymarks.) Through small wooden gate onto bridleway between high hedges.

(D) Soon turn left into grassy lane with tall hedges on either side. As this drops into valley, lane becomes stony track and then tarmac road. Enter hamlet of Stafford's Green at bottom of hill and almost immediately go to right, through large gate into farmyard opposite small garage of house on left. Go straight ahead between two barrel-roofed barns leaving hard surface. Continue straight ahead through kissing gate and immediately turn half-right to go over sleeper bridge. Turn left immediately beyond bridge and continue across field with hedge on right and stream on left.

(E) Gradually veer away from hedge on right and aim for far left corner of field, but at about 50 yards before stile in cross-hedge, bear left to go over sleeper bridge. Up

bank beyond stream and immediately turn right to go over double stile. Cross long, park-like field with slopes up to left and stream down to right. Initially follow to immediate left of trees and bushes and, when Sandford Orcas Manor is visible ahead, veer slightly left, but keep right of small mound with trees. Lovely views of manor and church over to right. Beyond brow, aim for middle of village's roof tops, stile not visible until just short of it.

Cadbury Castle from the south

(F) Over stile opposite *The Old House* and turn left onto road in Sandford Orcas *(but turn right if you wish to visit church)*. *This quiet stone and thatch village below the hills takes the second half of its name, Orcas, from that of the Norman family of 'de Orescuily'. Its church, beautifully situated beside the manor house, has a partly restored interior containing attractive angel corbel figures, a little 13th-century font and a family chapel in its south side with an old linenfold screen and several interesting monuments. There is the base of an old cross in the churchyard, close to a fine gateway to the manor house. This delightful Ham Hill stone Tudor building (sometimes open) has fine panelling, furniture and pictures within and terraced gardens with topiary without.* Almost immediately go straight (SP - *Sherborne*), not right, past phone box on right, and again straight (SP - *Sherborne*), not left. Mitre Inn beyond on right. Walk with care through village along its narrow and quite dangerous lane, which is lined with stone cottages and pretty gardens and which winds south-east and then south for over half-a-mile.

(G) Turn left onto small surfaced lane by post box on left and *No Through Road* sign. Go up lane for 20 yards and through opening into field on left. Keep along field edge, with hedge on right, to gate. Through gate and go straight ahead across field, bearing slightly left, to another gate. Through gate and immediately turn right keeping close to hedge for 50 yards. Where hedge bears away to right keep straight on, aiming for dip in skyline, and after 300 yards pass hedge-end protruding into field from right. Continue on same line to stile at edge of wood. Over stile into wood following path bending first to left and then immediately right, up a short, steep slope onto forest track. Turn left onto track and follow it up hill. Track soon becomes path through bracken and nettles. Keep straight on and emerge onto golf course. Keep close to fence and hedge on left and continue until level with clubhouse. *Fine views from here, back (north) to Glastonbury Tor and the Mendips.* Squeeze between clubhouse buildings and hedge on left.

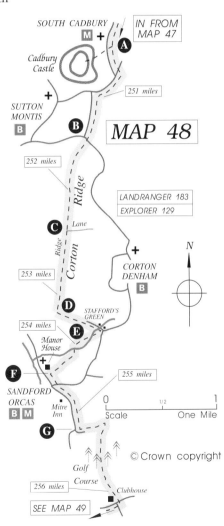

© Crown copyright

(A) Pass through clubhouse gate onto road. *Good views southwards to Woolland Hill and Bulbarrow Hill, with its masts.* Turn right along road down hill 600 yards to turn left at T-junction of roads (SP - *Sherborne*). Down road with strip lynchets (ancient cultivation terraces) visible on hillside to right.

(B) After half-a-mile, turn left beneath beech tree onto possibly obscured bridleway track known as Quarr Lane. Follow track, overhung with trees as it climbs, but turn left where it meets hedge at what looks like T-junction of paths. Continue up hill between hedges and after curious twists and turns, track becomes more purposeful and runs down hill in south-easterly direction. *Linger at second gate on right for panoramic view of Sherborne and hills beyond.* Quarr Lane's surface changes to tarmac and then becomes a road.

(C) Now enter outskirts of Sherborne, passing bungalows on left with well-kept gardens, and further beyond on right, a large depression, once a quarry, the source of much of old Sherborne's stone (hence 'Quarr Lane'). At Mermaid Hotel avoid road which runs past it (Blackberry Lane) and go half left, to immediate left of Mermaid Cottage, to join B3145, Bristol Road. Follow this down hill to traffic lights on the busy A30. Do not try to cross here, but bear right onto A30 and use pedestrian traffic lights just along to right, opposite Antelope Hotel.

(D) Having crossed A30, bear left down Higher Cheap Street. Continue down hill into Cheap Street by White Hart. Take care here as Cheap Street has one-way traffic coming down hill from behind you on both sides of road.

Sherborne is perhaps the most beautiful of all Dorset towns, so do take time off to explore its wealth of old buildings from every period. The Abbey, in the very heart of the town, was founded in AD705 by King Ine of Wessex. Visually the present building dates from the 15th century, following a disastrous fire in 1437, although it incorporates much of the Norman church built by Bishop Roger of Caen in about 1120. Sherborne Old Castle, to the east of the town, was also the work of Bishop Roger, but

like so many other English castles, it was largely destroyed during the Civil War. All that remains is the Norman gatehouse and portions of the keep, chapel and curtain walls. The nearby, 'new' Sherborne Castle, first built by Sir Walter Raleigh in 1594, contains fine furniture, porcelain and pictures and stands beside a lake in a 20-acre park landscaped by Capability Brown.

Pass archway on left leading to supermarket. Pass Post Office with phones on left, then archway on left leading to Swan Yard and toilets. On right at lower end of Cheap Street pavement broadens to form 'The Parade', where 'The Conduit' stands. *This is an hexagonal 16th-century building which originally stood in the cloisters on the north side of the Abbey, where it served as a washing place for the monks. It was moved to its present site after the dissolution of Sherborne's monastery in 1539.* This is probably the best access point for the Abbey, just beyond.

Sherborne Abbey

(E) A short way past the Conduit follow road round to right (westwards) where it becomes Half Moon Street. *But turn left up Long Street if you wish to visit Sherborne Old Castle and Sherborne Castle (see previous page).* After 100 yards pass Abbey on right and Digby Road down to left - Tourist Information Centre visible on right of Digby Road, and Police Station on its left, with Railway Station at end. A few yards beyond entry to Digby Road follow one-way system round to left, where Half Moon Street becomes Westbury (SP - *Yeovil*) - this is opposite 15th-century St Johns Almshouses on right. Continue along Westbury to traffic island, where road joins A352, Dorchester road, coming in from right. Follow A352 (SP - *Dorchester*) as it bends to left by factory entrance on left (SP - *Dorchester*) and climbs to cross railway and River Yeo. Castle ruins just visible down valley to left.

(F) After another 200 yards turn right at X-rds crossing A352 with very great care to go on smaller road (SP - *Thornford*). Great care should also be taken along this road. After 200 yards beyond x-rds, and beyond entrance to Limekiln Farm on left, go straight (SP - *Thornford*), not left. Go along left-hand side of road and after 100 yards, where road bends to right, turn left through kissing gate and over stile. Go up often muddy lane with hedge on each side and over stile beside farm gate. Go half right for about 30 yards over rough ground to fence. Bear left to keep this fence on right and small copse on left and continue up hill. Into rough field beyond copse and keep fence on right as far as waymarked corner post.

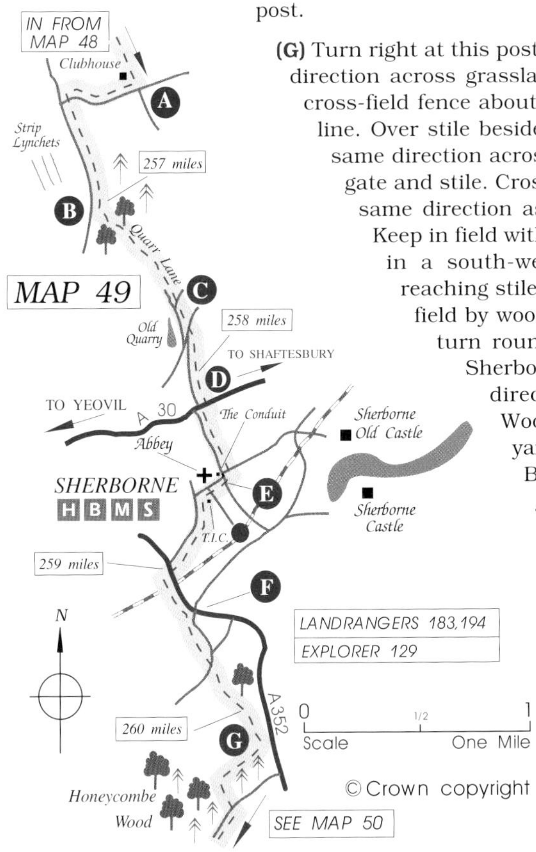

(G) Turn right at this post and head in southerly direction across grassland, aiming for stile in cross-field fence about 100 yards below tree-line. Over stile beside gate and continue in same direction across next field to another gate and stile. Cross stile and continue in same direction as far as edge of wood. Keep in field with wood on left, heading in a south-westerly direction until reaching stile in far, upper corner of field by wood. Before crossing stile turn round to take last look at Sherborne. Over stile leading directly into Honeycombe Wood and after about 20 yards, past old wicket gate. Bear left onto track and go almost due south, up hill through wood, and shortly over stile to emerge onto road. *Opposite, on other side of road, is a gate with fine view of central Dorset, with the masts on the skyline identifying Bulbarrow Hill, eleven miles to the south-east.*

IN FROM MAP 48

Clubhouse

Strip Lynchets

257 miles

Quarr Lane

MAP 49

Old Quarry

258 miles

TO SHAFTESBURY

TO YEOVIL   30

The Conduit

Sherborne Old Castle

Abbey

SHERBORNE

H B M S

Sherborne Castle

T.I.C.

259 miles

N

LANDRANGERS 183,194

EXPLORER 129

260 miles

A352

0   1/2   1
Scale   One Mile

© Crown copyright

Honeycombe Wood

SEE MAP 50

(A) Emerge from wood and turn right to follow minor road south-westwards with care. This is not busy but has many blind bends and it is best to walk on outside of all bends. After almost three-quarters-of-a-mile, turn sharp left at road junction (SP - *Lillington*). At bottom of hill, in small village of Lillington, bear round to right. *But turn left if you wish to visit the largely 13th- and 15th-century church with its sympathetically restored interior.* Pass fine stone barn and phone box on left.

(B) After about 500 yards reach grassy triangle where road turns sharply right up hill. Ignore this, cross triangle and continue southwards along track bordered by high hedges. Where right-hand hedge ends, go half-right through gate and aim diagonally (south-westwards) for top left-hand corner of field, aiming for large solitary oak tree on skyline. Just before corner, at highest point of field, over stile on right in wide hedge, over sleeper bridge and second stile. (Caution: between these two stiles is deep ditch bridged by single sleeper, which may sometimes be concealed by dense undergrowth.) Now aim half-left across field for stile a few yards to right of aforesaid oak tree, still dominating skyline. Cross stile and continue on same line aiming for gap in opposite hedge between willow to left and oak to right. Cross two stiles in this gap and continue in same direction (approximately south-westwards) aiming slightly to left of far corner of field, although gate not yet visible, being initially hidden by corner of hedge to left.

(C) Go through gate and turn right onto road. Go along and up road (west) for 400 yards to road junction. Continue in same direction for 25 yards while passing Higher Knighton Farm on left and turn left over stile in hedge. *Now entering the fringes of Blackmoor Vale, which was named 'The Vale of the Little Dairies' by the great Dorset novelist, Thomas Hardy. There is much rich pasture country to be crossed before we reach the coast, although today there are fewer milking herds and more beef cattle to be seen.* Down across small field, through gate and go diagonally right across next field to gate. Through gate and go diagonally right, across field aiming to right of single tree.

(D) Beyond tree go through gate to cross often muddy track known as Knighton Lane and through gate opposite. Go diagonally left to tip of wood on right known as Tibbles Copse, veer slightly to left, and go through gate and over farm bridge crossing stream. Continue across field aiming for double-stile to left of single tree in hedge. Over double-stile and go slightly left following waymark direction across field and aiming for metal gate to left of two trees in field. Through gate and across field to stile and gate in hedge to right of water trough.

(E) Over stile and go diagonally right across field aiming slightly to left of Yetminster church (just visible on skyline ahead). Go through another gate to left of metal water-trough and cross corner of field aiming for gate in side hedge with feed silo beyond. Through metal gate and along left-hand edge of field with farm building just beyond hedge. Cross exit lane from Westfield Farm buildings on left. Continue to stile with sleeper across possible mud patch beyond. Cross field to stile in opposite hedge and into Yetminster playing-fields. Follow hedge, going behind sports pavilion and then go down drive past allotments on right. Go through metal gate, pass re-cycling site on right, keep children's playground on left until exit into Brierley Hay. Turn right to meet village road in

Lane beyond Lillington

Some of Yetminster's delightful old houses

Brister End, Yetminster and turn right along it.

(F) *Over railway bridge and bear left to continue towards Yetminster centre, with railway station and Railway Inn to right. Yetminster is a large village lying in low country and possessing a wealth of interesting old houses, of which no fewer than 31 are 'listed buildings'. The tall tower of the handsome 13th- to 15th-century church has some fine gargoyles and a golden weathercock. Its bright interior is full of interest, with painted wagon-roof, 16th-century benches, a Norman font and some good monuments. Benjamin Jesty, probably the first man to vaccinate using cowpox, lived here in the 18th century and his descendants still live locally. More recently the Yetties Folk Group were all born here and still often play at village occasions.* Pass Manor Farm Guest House on right and turn left at triangle by Oak House Stores into Church Street (but go straight ahead up High Street if you wish to visit Post Office, telephone box, rest of useful shops or White Hart Inn). Pass Old School and Old Library on left, new Rectory, Village Hall and church on right. *Just beyond church is Sexton's Cottage, dated 1736. The farm on the right with large iron gates is Upbury, oldest house in the village and once the home of Benjamin Jesty.*

(G) By clipped yew tree at junction with Mill Lane and Birch Lane, take path to left of tree and through kissing gate. Go diagonally right uphill, across field to stile in high hedge. Down steps onto road, turn left and continue southwards down hill with great care, to go straight across at road junction (SP - *Melbury Osmond). (In very wet weather, you may be advised to keep on the road to Melbury Osmond (see Map 51, Page 117),* but take great care - traffic can be dangerous). Through stile beside next gate on left and turn right to continue in same line, parallel with road. Over stile in fence where field narrows, start to cross to left-hand hedge and follow it to metal gate and stile in field corner.

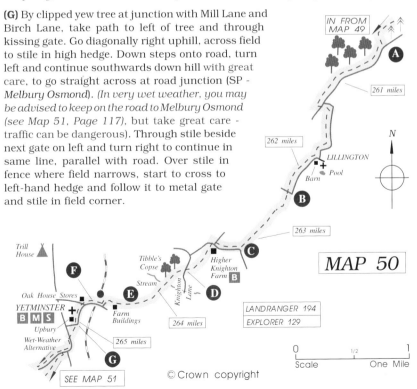

IN FROM MAP 49

261 miles

262 miles

LILLINGTON

Barn · Pool

N

B

263 miles

MAP 50

Trill House

F

Tibble's Copse

Higher Knighton Farm B

Stream

Knighton Lane

D

C

Oak House Stores

YETMINSTER
B M S

E

Farm Buildings

264 miles

Upbury

LANDRANGER 194

EXPLORER 129

Wet-Weather Alternative

265 miles

G

0 — 1/2 — 1
Scale   One Mile

SEE MAP 51

© Crown copyright

115

(A) Over stile and cross Horsehill Lane slightly left to go over sleeper bridge and stile in opposite hedge. Turn left, pass gateway on left, follow left-hand hedge and go over high stile beside water trough. Keep between hedge and rope/wire fence (livery stables over to right). At next cross-hedge go over sleeper and two stiles. Cross next small field in same direction and go over sleeper bridge and two consecutive stiles. Now go diagonally left to cut corner of large, long field to hedge and go over two stiles with long, wooden step between them. Cross next field to water trough in opposite hedge and turn right to walk with hedge on left. Follow this hedge to find stile below and to immediate right of large oak tree. Over stile and keep to right of hedge but detour right around outside of small fenced off area with pond and resume route alongside hedge to meet metal gate and stile into lane.

(B) Over stile by gate and turn right into Woodville Lane, rutted and sometimes muddy, but delightful in high summer, with overhanging trees and bushes. Where lane turns sharp right, go straight ahead through gate and follow waymark direction along right-hand hedge, but cut left across far corner of field and go over stile beside metal gate in hedge. Take short path to lane. Turn left here, onto stony path and bridge-like, concrete-covered drain keeping to middle of path to new gate. Through gate and uphill slightly left to head almost due south, aiming, when you spot it, for a single oak tree outside a wood known as Chetnole Withy Bed. Continue keeping wood on left as far as cross-field hedge. Then turn left into wood/scrub (do **not** go through small gate to right). Cross sleeper causeway across boggy area to stile by old metal gate.

(C) Go over this stile and along lush green-lane which runs within wood, until turning right (south) through metal gate into field. Traces of lane have vanished, although once known as Starveacre Lane. Follow hedge on left to cross-field hedge, and just before reaching this gated hedge, ignore stile to left. Go ahead through metal gate and continue to follow hedge and ditch on left until reaching another cross-hedge. Turn right and after a few yards go left through wide gap into remains of old lane. Turn right and enter drove-road ignoring farm lane going south to Manor Farm. Continue along drove-road which eventually opens out. Keep to left-hand corner to cross narrow stream. This is fordable, but is often muddy. Go into field through gap and continue south-westwards with hedge on left. Leave field through old metal gate and garden of Rest and Welcome Inn is on right.

(D) Walk to the right (northwards) past the inn, cross busy A37 with great care and continue along verge for 100 yards. *(This is the point where the Main Route is joined by the Wet-Weather Alternative, which uses roads from Yetminster - see Maps 50 and 51.)* Go over stile in left-hand hedge, then along field edge with hedge on left for about 200 yards and then go diagonally downhill across field to right-hand corner keeping well to left of farm buildings. Over stile in wire fence and turn right onto estate drive. At end of estate drive, turn left onto road in Drive End and follow road westwards, going over two flat bridges. Turn left into parking space beside second thatched cottage on left and remain in parking area to go behind cottage and through single gate. Follow tarmac path to The Meads, a lane leading to Melbury Osmond village street south of the church. *Melbury Osmond is a delightful stone and thatch village, very much part of the great Ilchester Estate (see below). The ill-fated Duke of*

Our entry to Melbury Park

Monmouth is reputed to have stopped here, the cottage in question being named after him. Thomas Hardy re-named the village King's Hintock *in his novels and it was in St Osmond's Church that both his grandparents and his parents were married. At that time the church must have had a pleasant Georgian flavour, but it was thoroughly 'restored' in 1888 and its only really noteworthy feature is a strange 10th- or 11th-century stone carving which may represent 'Abraham's ram caught in a thicket'.*

(E) Turn left onto village street (but turn right to visit church or use telephone box or bus shelter). Go past attractive watersplash and along road to Town's End. Pass Monmouth Cottage on left and follow road as far as gates of Melbury Park. Turn right here into small picnic area and then over stile onto estate drive (or go through gates if open). Follow this drive southwards through parkland for about three-quarters-of-a-mile to Melbury House.

(F) Turn right following drive around right-hand side of Melbury House and then south again through further delightful parkland. *The principal seat of the Fox-Strangways family, the Earls of Ilchester, Melbury House, together with the adjoining church, makes up the 'village' of Melbury Sampford, situated in the large and very beautiful deer park through which we are walking. The massive, rambling house* (not open to visitors) *was built by Giles Strangways in the 16th century but has been considerably altered and added to in the 17th and 19th centuries. The fine Tudor hexagonal tower, possibly intended as a point from which to observe deer hunting in the great park, is its most interesting feature. The church contains a large number of monuments commemorating members of the Strangways family.*

(G) After about a mile, leave park through main entrance and eventually pass large house on right just before bearing right onto road at entry to Evershot by triangular green known as 'The Common'. Head towards village centre passing village hall on left and Rectory House Hotel on right. *Standing at a surprising 700 feet above sea level, Evershot is Dorset's second highest village. Several bow-fronted windows look out from stone and thatch cottages across its attractive, sloping main street. The friendly Acorn Inn was renamed the 'Sow and Acorn' by Thomas Hardy in* Tess of the d'Urbervilles *and in this novel Tess breakfasts at the cottage next to the church. The latter building was much restored in the 19th century. Beyond it lies St John's Well, the source of the River Frome.*

Take next turn to left (SP - *Rampisham*) (but go straight ahead for Acorn Inn, church and phone box). This is part of the **Macmillan Abbotsbury-Langport Link**, which enables walkers to go coast-to-coast from Abbotsbury to Barnstaple.

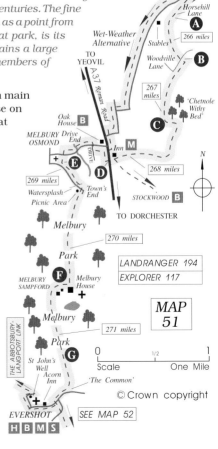

IN FROM
MAP 50

Horsehill
Lane

A

266 miles

Wet-Weather
Alternative

Stables

Woodville
Lane

B

TO
YEOVIL

A37 Roman Road

267
miles

'Chetnole
Withy
Bed'

C

Oak
House **B**

MELBURY
OSMOND

Drive
End

DRIVE

Inn **M**

268 miles

N

E

D

269 miles

Watersplash

Town's
End

STOCKWOOD **B**

Picnic Area

TO DORCHESTER

Melbury

270 miles

Park

LANDRANGER 194

EXPLORER 117

MELBURY
SAMPFORD

F

Melbury
House

MAP
51

Melbury

271 miles

THE ABBOTSBURY-LANGPORT LINK

Park

G

St John's
Well

0   1/2   1

Acorn
Inn

Scale   One Mile

'The Common'

© Crown copyright

EVERSHOT

SEE MAP 52

H **B** **M** **S**

(A) Having turned first left in Evershot, pass school on left and soon turn left off road, through metal gate opposite entrance to Summer Lodge Hotel. Cross field diagonally southwards and uphill, through gateway in left-hand hedge in field corner and turn right immediately through another gateway. Turn left and follow hedge on left. Cross farm lane and eventually turn left through gateway where hedgeline changes. Then turn right immediately and continue in former direction with hedge now on right. Go through gate in field corner and bear slightly left (south-eastwards) across field to metal gate and exit onto farm drive. Continue in same direction down driveway, passing farm cottages on left, then Fortuneswood Farmhouse on right and finally veer left of dutch barn.

(B) Go through gate and then south-eastwards along farm track with wire fence on left and hedge to right, with farm buildings behind it. At end of hedge go through metal gate on right and then through left-hand of two metal gates, going into narrow corner of fenced field. Follow left-hand fence until it turns left, then head south-eastwards downhill aiming for metal gate in field by corner of small spinney. Through this gate and aim for stile in fence beyond often boggy area with stream. Over stile and continue in same direction to left of oak tree to field corner. Bear left (eastwards) through metal gate into beginning of farm track. Follow this track (but cut diagonally to right, across corner if too wet), until reaching surfaced area of Chantmarle, once a police training college.

(C) Turn right (SW) at entry to Chantmarle, continue along roadway past storehouse and training tower on right and some houses on left. Bear left, up across rough ground with trees and soon go through small gate on right below power-pole into field. Turn right cutting off corner of field and then turn left along hedge. Follow to left of hedge with wooded hollow to left and where hedge turns sharp right, bear half-left across field aiming for right-hand end of woodlands in hollow ahead. Go through gate just within right-hand end of woodlands onto farm drive.

(D) Cross drive, going slightly right, to go through gate. North Holway Farm visible to left. Go almost straight across field to gate in middle of hedge. Through gate and continue in same direction across narrow corner of field and through two consecutive gates. Keep straight across large field and through gate in hedge into next field, turning left, then right, to go with hedge to immediate left. Follow this hedge to Holway Farm and go through right-hand of two gates keeping to right of farm buildings. Veer left at end of buildings and silage area, to go down field to gate in field corner and exit at lane's junction with road.

Cattistock Church

(E) Turn left (southwards) down road and turn left at road junction by grassy triangle (SP - *Cattistock*) to go over bridge across railway line, and enter hamlet of Sandhills just beyond. Keep on road through Sandhills hamlet (SP - *Cattistock*). Enter Cattistock and just beyond Post Office Stores on right and just before Fox and Hounds Inn on left, go into churchyard. *Described as 'elbow-street Cattistock' by the 19th-century Dorset poet, William Barnes, this attractive little village nestling in the upper valley of the River Frome, still has its 19th-century houses grouped around a sharp hairpin bend near the church. Most of this was rebuilt in 1857 by Sir Gilbert Scott, but the splendidly pinnacled tower was added by his son, George, in 1874. The screened-off baptistry beneath the tower, contains a font with an* impressive cover, all of 20 feet high, and makes a visit here worthwhile.

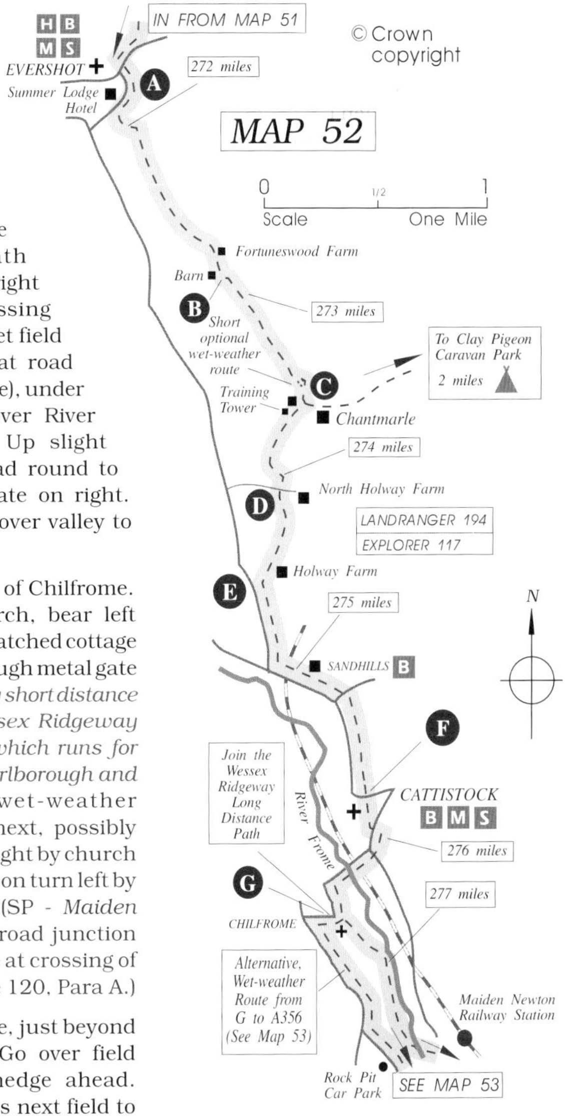

(F) Keep to left of church and follow path down to metal gate, passing ornate sunken spring down to left. Continue along fenced path southwards and turn right onto road, soon passing beautifully sited cricket field on right. Turn right at road junction (SP - Chilfrome), under railway bridge and over River Frome just beyond. Up slight incline and follow road round to left by wide, white gate on right. Pleasant views to left over valley to hills beyond.

(G) Soon enter hamlet of Chilfrome. On approaching church, bear left down track between thatched cottage and church-yard, through metal gate and into field. *For a very short distance we now join the Wessex Ridgeway Long Distance Path, which runs for 137 miles between Marlborough and Lyme Regis.* (In wet-weather conditions, to avoid next, possibly flooded section, turn right by church keeping on road and soon turn left by houses in Chilfrome (SP - *Maiden Newton*). Fork left at road junction and re-join main route at crossing of A356 on Map 53 (Page 120, Para A.)

(G) Back on main route, just beyond Chilfrome Church - Go over field aiming for gap in hedge ahead. Through gap and cross next field to

MAP 52

IN FROM MAP 51

272 miles

EVERSHOT
Summer Lodge Hotel

Fortuneswood Farm

Barn

273 miles

Short optional wet-weather route

Training Tower

Chantmarle

To Clay Pigeon Caravan Park

2 miles

274 miles

North Holway Farm

LANDRANGER 194

EXPLORER 117

Holway Farm

275 miles

SANDHILLS

N

Join the Wessex Ridgeway Long Distance Path

River Frome

CATTISTOCK

276 miles

277 miles

CHILFROME

Alternative, Wet-weather Route from G to A356 (See Map 53)

Maiden Newton Railway Station

Rock Pit Car Park

SEE MAP 53

unusual stile. Cross stile, turn left and follow hedge on left. Go round crop if cultivated and over stile on left into water meadows. Head towards wooded area and turn right when reaching River Frome. Follow this through attractive area with pleasant water-based vegetation and many different species of trees, including alder, willow, beech, ash and hazel. Go under railway arch, which carried now defunct Maiden Newton - Bridport branch line, and continue in lush vegetation. Pass buildings above on left, with several private bridges. Cross waymarked public footbridge on left and follow path winding slightly upwards, through dark, damp clearing emerging into a field.

(A) Follow up path to left of church and turn right onto road into Maiden Newton. Pass war memorial on left, turn right into centre of village and turn right again onto A356. Cross River Frome and, where minor road comes in from right, turn left to cross busy A356 with great care. (The Wet-Weather Alternative comes in here.) Now leave road to cross footbridge ahead next to village noticeboard. Bear slightly left across field to go through two kissing gates in corner. Follow path beside River Frome until reaching metal gate on left. Through gate and turn right onto lane.

(B) Soon turn right (SP - *Cruxton*) near Frome Vauchurch church (which is ahead on left). *The small church here was much restored in 1870, but some of its Norman and Early English features were retained and its contents include a Jacobean pulpit. There are also pleasant old tabletop tombs in its little tree-shaded churchyard.* Soon turn left at next road junction (SP - *Cruxton*).

(C) Through Cruxton hamlet where tarmac road becomes track. Follow track uphill through field (SP - *Notton*). Follow sign on right directing us left. Soon turn right (SP - *Compton Valence*) and go on concrete roadway (with hedge on right) which eventually becomes unsurfaced track. At top of hill do not go through fenced opening (single wire) ahead, but turn left and after few yards turn right through opening in hedge. Continue across long field with hedge on immediate right and at corner, where there is a wooden sign, turn left still keeping hedge on right. Over stile in corner of field and bear right, downhill, across field towards clump of trees.

(D) Aim for gate to left of Notton Hill Barn complex, go through this gate and turn right down lane past buildings on right. Through two metal gates, down one slope and up the next, with attractive open views on both sides. Continue to end of furthest field on ridge with hedge on right - the last part of this route is on grass - do not follow any track to right. When reaching corner of field note three gates on right and wooden sign. Go through all three and turn left (SP - *Compton Valence*). With hedge now on left continue down slope on grassy track towards Compton Bottom. Compton Valence now visible ahead. Go through metal gate bearing right along track with beautiful views of green and unspoilt valley. Keep following track which bears sharp right. On reaching valley floor with its badger setts, go through gate where two fences on left meet at right-angles. Continue down green slope across field, bearing right of solitary tree.

(E) Keep bearing right, go through gate in corner of field and turn right onto well defined track. Soon pass farm buildings and converted barns before emerging onto road in minute village of Compton Valence. Turn right, past phone box on right and then turn left opposite small Victorian church onto surfaced lane (and not through gate to its right into

Downland track to Compton Valence

woods). Go along and then up lane through pleasant woodlands of Compton Valence House, with attractive gardens and pond on right. Follow lane round to right and by small garage-like building on left, carry straight ahead and up through metal gate where lane bears to left. Go up pleasant, shaded green lane.

(F) Just beyond top of hill bear left into field. Now continue southwards, with hedge on immediate left. Attractive views to left down into dry valley. Go over double stile at end of field and turn left to go down minor road which follows course of possible Roman Road. After about 50 yards, turn right off road, through first metal gate and immediately through second gate in hedge to left. Go along field keeping to immediate left of hedge-line. Through metal gate in next hedge-line and into large meadow. Go downhill keeping to left of hedge, then up, and under high-voltage power-line.

(G) *At this point we cross a bridleway carrying the Dorset Jubilee Trail, a 90-mile regional path running westwards across the county from Forde Abbey to Bokerley Dyke, between Blandford and Salisbury. Good views ahead of ridge beyond Bride Valley, with Hardy Monument clearly visible on left (in memory of Admiral Hardy, Nelson's 'Captain Hardy' at Trafalgar).* Carry on southwards, through metal gate, to clump of trees ahead. Follow track downwards to Kingston Russell Farm, joining lane through farmyard and then forking right along surfaced lane to A35. Cross very busy A35 with great care and through metal hunting gate to right of concrete farm road and onto this farm road to go gently up hill.

(H) Turn left near storage pit, through metal gate and follow to immediate left of fence-line going gently uphill to end of field. Through hunting gate below small, wind-bent hawthorn tree and immediately turn right. *Note to left of hawthorn tree, small round-barrow topped by a boulder – probably part of its original burial chamber. Lovely pastoral views over the Bride Valley ahead and to a ridge in the distance beyond.*

IN FROM MAP 52

Wet-weather alternative

TO CREWKERNE

Rock Pit Car Park

MAIDEN NEWTON

H B M S

Wessex Ridgeway

A 356

A

278 miles **B**

FROME VAUCHURCH

MAP 53

CRUXTON

C

River Frome

TO DORCHESTER

279 miles

280 miles

D Notton Hill Barn

LANDRANGER 194

EXPLORERS OL15, 117

281 miles **E**

N

Compton Valence House

COMPTON VALENCE

F 282 miles

Roman Road

Dorset Jubilee Trail

G

Kingston Russell Farm

TO BRIDPORT

A35

To Newhaven, Winterbourne Steepleton 2 miles

283 miles

H TO DORCHESTER

Storage Pit

284 miles

SEE MAP 54

Round Barrow

0 1/2 1

Scale

One Mile

(A) Go through metal gate with wire fence on right (SP - *Bridleway to Whatcombe*) and down pleasant sunken lane with, in high summer, many butterflies and the scent of camomile. Beware of deep ruts in track. *Kingston Russell House visible in valley well ahead right. This elegant 16th- and 18th-century house stands on the site of what was once the home of the Russell family, the forbears of the Dukes of Bedford.* Pass unusual modern, `period' house on right, but pleasant views to left of ridges and downland.

(B) At bottom of hill cross minor road with care, in view of sharp left-hand bend just to right. Go through wooden gate onto path. This eventually narrows and hedges on both sides soon become thicker and taller, and path appears to follow bed of stream. Kingston Russell House lies beyond thick hedge on right. Despair not if things seem jungly, as path suddenly emerges into pleasant, small grassy water-meadow. Bear round to right and through gate with house on right. Then turn left, over footbridge across little River Bride beside ford and along well surfaced drive.

(C) Go through drive's gate and up road ahead. Three telegraph poles on, where a track goes sharp-left, go half-left through kissing gate into field. Head diagonally across field passing power-pole, going over insulated fence and through gate bearing right. Good views back to ridge, with Whatcombe House prominent on hill to right. Keep in lee of wood on right and then turn right through hunting gate on right. Traverse wood (path often boggy - possibly go parallel, slightly to right of path) and soon emerge into field through hunting gate. Continue in same direction across field and through metal gate. Go ahead slightly uphill, through metal gate and after looking to the right for a distant view of Lyme Bay (Yes - the sea at last!), head for next gate, which has a venerable sycamore tree behind it.

Abbotsbury ahead!

(D) Go through gate and bear diagonally left up well-defined track. Pass thin hedge of tall hawthorn trees on left and then turn left to go over stile. Continue in same direction diagonally (south-eastwards) across next field (Tenants Hill) and over brow to its far corner where stands the Kingston Russell Stone Circle (sometimes partly hidden by growing crop). *This Bronze Age stone circle has 18 low stones and stands at a point where five public footpaths converge. There are splendid all-round views from here.*

(E) Go through metal gate on right, in corner of field just beyond stone circle, and follow to immediate right of hedge-line, going south-westwards. Through next gate and note attractive view of valley and, to right, the sea below Golden Cap, some miles to the west, beyond Bridport. Continue downhill towards wooded area on left. Go through metal gate, bear right, round back of cottages and then left through gate onto lane. Go past cottages, through Gorwell Farm and along surfaced road through pleasant wooded area.

(F) At end of wooded area on right, where private road bears left, turn right through gate to go up hill along concrete path with hedge on right. Pass first metal gate where concrete path becomes track and then, after short distance, go through second metal gate. Now follow to immediate left of wire fence across field. *Soon come to highest point of rounded White Hill, with its splendid views over Abbotsbury to the sea, including the long line of Chesil Bank with the lagoons of the Fleet on its landward side, and the peninsula of Portland Bill beyond to the east.*

(G) Go down hill on bridleway keeping to left of signpost indicating inland alternative of South-West Coast Path, which we cross. Now on limestone terrace, part of old quarry workings and a good place to stop awhile. *The limestone in the quarries is part of the same family group of oolite over which the Macmillan Way has been passing since it left the Fens at Kate's Bridge, some 260 miles to the north-east. Much of the village of Abbotsbury still lies hidden below and beyond the brow, but the very satisfying view covers, from right - White Nothe Cliff, Weymouth Bay, Isle of Portland, Chesil Bank, the Fleet, and directly ahead, in the near distance - the Swannery, St Catherine's Chapel and just below it, Abbotsbury's church and tithe barn.* Now go through metal gate to left. Pass signpost to Abbotsbury and an interesting notice regarding old quarry workings and continue down hill with Abbotsbury coming into view. Go through metal gate and follow track bearing left and noting strip lynchets just ahead to right. Continue down hill passing signpost to Abbotsbury on left and through metal gate into grassy, rocky lane (very slippery in wet weather - *evidence of ironstone which was once quarried here and taken by rail to Weymouth for shipping out from there*). Lane narrows to a path and drops steeply, going round to left, then right into Abbotsbury village.

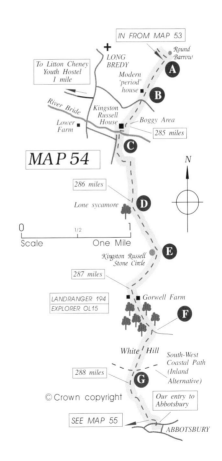

IN FROM MAP 53

Round Barrow

LONG BREDY

To Litton Cheney Youth Hostel 1 mile

Modern 'period' house

River Bride

Kingston Russell House

Lower Farm

Boggy Area

285 miles

MAP 54

N

286 miles

Lone sycamore

0   1/2   1

Scale   One Mile

Kingston Russell Stone Circle

287 miles

LANDRANGER 194
EXPLORER OL15

Gorwell Farm

White Hill

South-West Coastal Path (Inland Alternative)

288 miles

© Crown copyright

Our entry to Abbotsbury

SEE MAP 55

ABBOTSBURY

Abbotsbury is an unspoilt stone and thatch village amidst partly wooded downland country just inland from the sea, where Chesil Beach joins the mainland. Its Benedictine Abbey was founded in the 11th century by Orc, King Canute's chief steward and flourished for 500 years before being largely demolished following the Dissolution of the Monasteries in 1539. The remaining ruins are not over-exciting, but the splendid 14th-century tithe barn, now known as The Smugglers' Barn, is well worth a visit. The nearby parish church is also full of interest, including an unusual plastered and barrel-vaulted chancel ceiling and a fine Jacobean pulpit. Standing by itself on a little hill just to the south-west of the village, and on our route, is the little St Catherine's Chapel. Also barrel-vaulted and stoutly buttressed, this was built by the monks of Abbotsbury in the 14th century as a landmark for sailors. On the shore of the Fleet, almost due south of St Catherine's, is Abbotsbury's best known feature - The Swannery. First mentioned as early as 1393, it has, like the rest of Abbotsbury, been in the hands of the Strangways family since the Dissolution. The swans stay here because there is a plentiful supply of their favourite food growing in the Fleet, a type of seaweed known as Zostera Marina. In sheltering woods well to the west of the village is Abbotsbury's other well known feature - The Sub-Tropical Gardens, which are possibly best visited after your conclusion of the Macmillan Way (see below). Originally laid out in the 18th century, these gardens are well sheltered from the sea and usually frost-free. Consequently many exotic plants are to be found here, in addition to palms, bamboos, camellias, rhododendrons and azaleas.

(A) Turn right onto minor road in Abbotsbury and, just beyond phone box on right, bear right onto B3157 by Post Office and Ilchester Arms, keeping in same, westerly direction (but turn left if you wish to visit Church, Tithe Barn or Swannery). Cross to south side of road and turn left at first lane (sign - *St Catherine's Chapel*), between pottery and Chapel Lane Stores. *This busy shop is almost always open and it is hoped that you will call in to record your completion of the Macmillan Way (or of part of it) in the Record Book kept here. However if you also require a response from us would you please write to us at the address below. Do not expect an ecstatic welcome here - your arrival richly deserves it but it is a routine to them, and it is good of them to hold our book for us. We hope you will understand.* This lane soon becomes a track and St Catherine's Chapel is visible on hill to right. Go through metal gate (SP - *St Catherine's Chapel*) and follow track up hill to St Catherine's Chapel.

(B) After visiting chapel drop down south-eastwards following permissive path over open field. Over stile with copse on left until reaching stone sign on cross-track, which is southern option of South-West Coast Path. Turn right and follow South-West Coast Path's track to reach stile (SP - *Tropical Gardens*). Over stile and bear left, following South-West Coast Path. Chesil Beach is now ahead but path bears round to right and in just over half-a-mile arrive at Chesil Beach Car Park (Toilets).

(C) Go up and over the Chesil Beach on wooden footway to arrive at the sea-shore - and the end of your 290-mile-long journey along the Macmillan Way from Boston on the Lincolnshire coast.

Congratulations on completing your journey. We hope that you have enjoyed it all. If you would like a Certificate recording our congratulations on your achievement, please write to us

Abbotsbury Tithe Barn

St Catherine's Chapel, Abbotsbury

- The Macmillan Way Association, St Mary's Barn, Pillerton Priors, Warwick CV35 0PG.

If, at the same time, you feel like making a small contribution to Macmillan Cancer Relief, for the support of which the Macmillan Way was both established and is maintained, it would be much appreciated.

Your contribution will be forwarded to them without any deduction and your generosity and that of any possible sponsoring friends and relations will be acknowledged and, if you have requested one, a Certificate will also be supplied. For further details see page 7.

We should also be most interested to hear how you fared, so do drop us a line if you can spare a few moments. If, on the other hand, you are already setting out from Abbotsbury to Land's End on the South-West Coast Path, we shall not expect to hear from you for a week or so ! But whatever your next objective - Good Luck and Happy Walking.

Peter and Janet Titchmarsh

NOTE: THIS MAP IS TWICE THE NORMAL SCALE

MAP 55

LANDRANGER 194
EXPLORER OL15

Chapel Lane Stores
Check-in Point

IN FROM
MAP 54

A

ABBOTSBURY
H M B S

South-West
Coast Path
to Minehead

290 miles

Abbotsbury
Sub-Tropical
Gardens

South-West Coast Path

289 miles

St Catherine's
Chapel ✝ **B**

Abbey
Ruins

Tithe Barn

To Portesham
Dairy
Farm
2 miles

South-West
Coast Path
to Poole

C

Car Park
and Toilets

N

Swannery Shop
and Restaurant

Journey's End
. . 290 miles
from Boston

Chesil Beach

Abbotsbury
Swannery

The Fleet
(part of)

To Camp Sites at
Langton Herring,
Fleet, Bagwell
and Chickerell.
Between 3
and 6 miles

0   1/2
Scale   Half-a-Mile

© Crown
copyright

INDEX

ACKNOWLEDGEMENTS AND THANKS

Both this guide book and the Long Distance Path, which it describes, are the result of much work by many individual walkers and teams of walkers, and the invaluable help and advice of many others. We are especially indebted to the officers of the ten counties through which the Way passes, all of whom have shown patience, understanding and encouragement. Much of the route passes through the Cotswolds Area of Outstanding Natural Beauty and the Rangers and Wardens of the Cotswold Countryside Service have provided extra-ordinarily active support. Priscilla Houston, the originator of the Wessex Ridgeway Long Distance Path, has provided much advice and encouragement. Parish Clerks along the whole route have been most helpful in the provision of details on land occupancy throughout all 290 miles of the route.

But perhaps most significantly of all, we are very much indebted to the vast majority of the occupiers of the land over which the Macmillan Way passes, be they small tenant farmers, great private estate-owners, or public bodies like Forest Enterprises. With very few exceptions they have dealt with our enquiries and, some might feel, our intrusions, in a tolerant and friendly manner. Consequently this facet of our work has been a pleasure rather than a chore and we are now more than ever convinced that closer, more friendly contact between walker and land occupier can lead to a greater understanding of each other's points of view. Thank you to them all.

Inevitably we shall miss some names, but may we record our grateful thanks to those within the various categories named above, including the following:

Carl Abram, Alisdair and Jane Alexander-Orr, Hugh Angus, Lyn and Alan Arnold, Andy Bailey, David Ball, Noel Banks, Richard Barnard, Alan Bentley, Elizabeth Bingley, Mary Birchall, Sara Blyde, John Bird, Dennis Boyce, David Branson, Mike Brinkworth, Barbara Burke, Alan Burnett, Rob Bygrave, Andy Carroll, Eric and Stella Case, Anna Chamberlin, Michael and Elizabeth Chambers, Jeff Cherrington, John Clayton, Ray and Annabel Clifton, Bill Coleman, Tony Combridge, Mark Connelly, Giles Cooper, Jim Cosford, Geoff Cox, Tony Crocker, Ron Custis, Richard Cuthbert, Geoff Davis, Jack de Carteret, Dick Dellow, Ed Delve, Eric Doel, Lisa Dover, John Duguid, Mary Edwards, Bill and Pat Ellis, Douglas Ellis, Betty Evans and friends, Peter Evans, Jill Everett, Elaine Fletcher, Alan Francis, Frank Franklin, John French, Maurice Freeland, Lady Dawn Gamble, Alan Gibbon, John Gibson, Jim Gooding, Diana Goodison, Nigel Goodrich, Harry Green and friends, Tony Griffith, Bob Hadfield, Peter Harrison, David Hawkins, Colin Haywood, Tony Hewitt, Pat Hinksman, John Honnor, Peter Houthuesen, Wesley Hughes, Tim Humphreys, Stuart Ikeringill, Fran & Phil Jacklin, Lewis James, Maurice Johns, Andy Johnson, Peter Jones, Janet Lake, Violet Layzell, Malcomb Larby, Dick Lees, Philip Lees, Chris Lemon, Simon Levell, Peter Lewis, Tony Locke, Vi Lord, Colin Lovelock, Michael McGarvie, Eddie McWilliam, Alan and Kathleen Marshall, Bob Martin, George Mason, Kath May, David Moore, Ian Morley, John Morris, Philip Morris, Stephen Newbury, Hamish and Mary Nicol, Gerry Nield, Tom Norcross, John Norris, James Ogilvie, David O'Neil, Ian Paterson, Peter Peters, Sheila Petherbridge, Charlie Phelps, Eileen Phillips, Andrew Pike, Denise Pinner, Mike Plaskitt, Hugh Potter, Ralph Price, Val and Peter Pym, John Redshaw, Kathy Rees, Dave Reynolds, Colin Roberts, Harry Robinson, John Rogers, George Sandwith, Rebecca Simmons, Jane Slaymaker, Geoffrey Smith, Hilary Smith, John Sneddon, Barry Snell, Stephen Spencer, Judy Spring, Chris Spry, Karen Stew, Mark Stratton, Dave Street, Andrew Tasker, Maurice Tebbutt and friends, Robin Thring, Frances Toogood, Michael Toop, John Trusler, Rita Turner, Barry Twist, Sarah Videan, Sue Viner, John Waters, Andy Waywell, John Wilkey, Tony Wilson, Mike Wood, Bob Woodward, Derek Wythes and Tom Youngman.